33 WAYS

Other publications by Judith Doctor:

I Forgive You: How Heart-Based Forgiveness Sets You Free
Dream Treasure: Learning the Language of Heaven

33 WAYS

How to Unlock the Mystery of Your Dreams

If you seek her as silver, and search for her as for hidden treasures; then you will ... discover the knowledge of God (Proverbs 2:4,5).

Judith A. Doctor

Doctor Resources

33 Ways: How to Unlock the Mystery of Your Dreams

© 2018 Judith A. Doctor

Original edition, *Christian Dreamwork: 33 Ways To Discover Divine Treasure In Dreams*, copyright © 2014 by Gerald R. & Judith A. Doctor. (No significant changes have been made to the text as originally published.)

Published in the United States by
Doctor Resources
www.judithdoctor.com

Unless otherwise specified, Scripture taken from the New American Standard Bible, Copyright © 1960, 1962, 1963, 1968, 1971, 1972, 1973, 1975, 1977, 1995 by The Lockman Foundation. Used by permission. www.Lockman.org

ISBN: 978-0-9837917-7-5

Doctor Resources provides educational and inspirational publications and other resources that nurture Christian spiritual maturity and transformative growth through the Holy Spirit.

Editor, Designer, Producer: Gerald R. Doctor

Printed in the United States of America

To the brave and courageous, you who are willing to ask tough questions and look to see if God just might be behind your dreams—may you find great joy in discovering the hidden treasure in dreams.

Contents

Preface

In the Talmud, Rabbi Hisda said: "An uninterpreted dream is like an unread letter."[1] I like to think of our dreams as letters from God containing guidance, counsel, and instruction for our lives. My goal is to help God's people listen to their dreams and benefit from the divine treasure they contain.

Throughout the centuries, dreams have had tremendous influence on Christianity. They were part of orthodoxy from the earliest centuries of the Christian church. The Apostolic Fathers, early Apologists, and Doctors of the Church all valued dreams and visions, recognizing them as vehicles for God to communicate to His people. These leaders embraced a spiritual worldview that affirms the importance of dreams.

This was an accepted view down through the centuries, until the advent of rational Christianity that denied the value of this divine gift. Relegating dreams to the occult, superstition, or simply too much pizza, we have lost touch with dreams. Hearing from God through dreams has become a sadly neglected aspect of our Christian experience.

Christians today are dreaming powerful dreams, but few recognize their divine origin or know how to benefit from their hidden treasure. Unaware of the scriptural basis of dreams and the teaching of the Church Fathers on dreams, people simply ignore this wonderful gift from God.

How do dreams help us?

Dreams are powerful. They have motivational, inspirational, creative, curative, and transformative power, capable of charging us with great energy. Dreamers like Dr. A. J. Gordon[a] and Mother Teresa were empowered to do great things in their lives.

---

[a] Adoniram Judson Gordon (1836–1895) was an American Baptist preacher, writer, and composer who founded Gordon College and Gordon-Conwell Theological Seminary in Massachusetts.

Contemporary research shows the extraordinary significance of dreaming to human life. Recent studies validate the positive effects of dreaming on every dimension of our lives, including our outer life and inner world. Dreaming is essential to mental and physical health and our entire well-being.[2] Most Christians are unaware that science has chronicled the numerous benefits of dreaming and dream work.[3]

Baptist minister Herman Riffel[b] found that dreams help us realize every part of our potential and bring us into harmony with God, others, and ourselves. In unlocking the mystery of his dreams, he uncovered treasure buried in the vast ocean of our inner world, hidden from our natural mind.[4]

Anglican priest Terrence McGillicuddy[c] discovered that dreams have the power to move someone out of darkness and fear into light and hope. Dream work offers an opportunity to find inner healing, psychological transformation, and spiritual aliveness. Dreams are a source of spiritual insight into our lives, leading us to an *authentic and profound experience with God.*

Since the 1970s, sleep labs and dream research have established that dreaming is a universal phenomenon. Everyone dreams one to two hours every night. That's five years of dreaming in a typical lifetime.[5] As believers in Jesus Christ, we must challenge ourselves: How did we get this ability to dream? Was it given to us by our Creator? Why did He give it to us? Do we need to be afraid of any capacity God has given to us?

You can understand your dreams

My own story is a testimony to the power of working with our dreams. I became alert to dreams in the late 1970s, shortly after I became aware of the Holy Spirit. As I awoke in the morning, fragments of dreams floated into my mind. These dramatic narratives felt important, but I didn't know how to make sense of them.

At this critical juncture in my spiritual journey, God provided me

---

b Originally from a Mennonite background, the late Herman Riffel (1917-2009) served many years as a Baptist pastor before the Lord called him to travel and lecture on hearing the voice of God in dreams. He spoke in churches across all denominations in fifty countries. His audiences varied from analysts, psychologists and psychiatrists in Sydney, Australia, to priests, nuns and Gregorian University professors in Rome. Riffel authored several books on dreams.

c Dr. McGillicuddy, an Anglican priest and Christian psychotherapist, worked for 22 years as a hospice Chaplain. He published his findings in *Sacred Dreams & Life Limiting Illness: A Depth Psychospiritual Approach* (Bloomington, IN: WestBow Press, 2013), Kindle edition.

with wise mentors who were consciously embracing dreams in their own Christian experience. They brought dreams from the mystical realm down to the practical earthly level where I lived.

Although God speaks in many ways,[d] He often has communicated with me using dreams—to guide and counsel me, answer my prayers, heal and transform me, reveal my gifts and anointing, direct my ministry, give me spiritual revelation, and bring me into a more intimate relationship with Him. Decades of personal study and practical experience with my dreams (and counseling others with theirs) strengthen my conviction that dreams offer access to a wealth of hidden treasure for our lives.

Earlier I wrote *Dream Treasure: Learning the Language of Heaven* to pass on my discoveries about this neglected gift from God.[6] I wanted to provide the Christian community with a comprehensive resource manual on the Christian use of dreams. In that book, I establish the basis for dreams and dream work, grounding them in biblical Christianity and the teachings of the early Church Fathers. *Dream Treasure* provides a thoroughly Christian framework within which to safely approach dreams and discover their divine purpose.

Because working with the picture language of dreams can be difficult, I saw the need for a practical handbook to help make sense of your dreams. *33 Ways: How to Unlock the Mystery of Your Dreams* describes specific skills, strategies, and techniques to help you relate to your dreams.

Dream Interpretation tools

33 Ways offers you ideas on how to approach dreams, interact with their symbolic imagery, and make *felt connections*[e] to their meanings [i.e., the response in our spirit, the witness of the Holy Spirit, the "Aha!"]. The tools for working with dreams are drawn from many sources—the Bible, Church Fathers, Christian practices, dream research, dream authors, and my own wealth of experiences.

I emphasize that there is no single correct method or school of thought that we can apply methodically to every dream. Since there are many different types of dreams, you will need a variety of approaches to help you

---

d Christians living in the 21st century are privileged to hear from God in numerous ways. We can expect the Holy Spirit to communicate with us through spiritual practices such as prayer, the Bible, the Eucharist, praise, worship, meditation, and through our spiritual senses, intuitive knowing, spiritual thoughts, our faith, the charisma, prophecy, dreams and visions.
e Refers to the response in our spirit, the witness of the Holy Spirit, the "Aha." (See #6, *The "Aha!" Moment*)

interact with them. Just become familiar with an array of skills, strategies and techniques, then use the ones you are drawn toward.

Similarly, *33 Ways* does not offer a canned approach to interpreting dream symbols. Every symbolic image has many possible meanings and associations. I believe it's misleading to say *this* always means *that*. Instead I give you the *tools to discover* what your dream symbols mean to you in your own inner world.

I also highlight the importance of our spiritual senses, intuitive perception, and the role of the Holy Spirit as we work with our dreams. Knowing that we can learn much about understanding dreams from the experiences of others, I have enriched the book with many dreams—from the Bible, Church Fathers, dreamers through the centuries, and, naturally, my own.

When people become aware that God is speaking to them through dreams, they often have many questions. Do all dreams come from God? How can I know if a dream is divine or just a dream? Are all dreams equally important? How can I understand those bizarre images?

What about dreams of dying or dreams of sexual encounters? Can Satan give us dreams? What about nightmares? What should I do with dreams about other people? How can I know if my dream is for the whole body of Christ or only for me? How will I know if my dream is prophetic? Can the Lord use dreams to speak to people who don't have a close relationship with Him? This book answers questions like these, and many more.

How to use this handbook

You don't have to read hundreds of books to understand your dreams. I have collected and organized a wide variety of tools that make it easy to work with dreams. At the heart of this book are the bulleted lists of practical steps for working with dreams.

The material is organized into six parts to facilitate learning how to unlock the mystery of our dreams. I begin with basic skills and strategies, progress through ways that dreams relate to our daily life, and advance towards working with dream symbols that connect to our inner dynamics.

Note: The first time I quote or reference someone, I provide additional information about them in a footnote.

Part One: Fundamental Skills starts with the premise that listening to our dreams is based upon a spiritual worldview, acknowledging that dreams have a divine author. It introduces the fundamental skills and practices essential in beginning dream work.

Part Two: Nighttime Dramas presents fundamental concepts and principles that provide a Christian basis for valuing dreams. It describes the biblical purposes of dreams and the differing types of dreams likely to appear. This part also provides an understanding of symbolic language, the language that most dreams use.

Part Three: Dream Processing shows how to draw out the information already visible in a dream and relate it to events in everyday life. Using processing techniques, we can find connections between our heart and our outer life choices.

Part Four: Non-Interpretive Strategies begins by acknowledging that many dreams cannot be opened up intellectually or rationally. Meditative, intuitive, and imaginative strategies offer other ways to engage our dreams and discover more insights into them. This part explains how to bring our troubling dreams to God.

Part Five: Symbolic Techniques helps us explore a dream symbol and connect to its inner meaning using five steps. This is the heart of dream work: unlocking the meaning of a symbol in a dream. Also this part introduces some symbolic figures likely to appear in dreams, explains principles of testing an interpretation, and discusses the importance of responding to dreams.

Part Six: Dream Work for Healthcare Professionals provides people working in holistic health care with guidance on how to use dream work to help others benefit from their dreams.

On a lighter note, I hope you enjoy the imaginative encounters between God and biblical dreamers written by my husband, Gerald. Perhaps they will help you think in a new way about dreams and inspire you to interact with your own "letters from God."

Acknowledgements

Special thanks goes to Judith King (MSW), my friend and Christian therapist, for suggesting the need for a straightforward, practical book on working with dreams. I decided to develop a handbook that would simplify the process for people who want to understand their dreams, and also be a resource for healthcare professionals who help others with their dreams.

For valuable feedback on the manuscript, I thank Jackie Venegas (MSW), and also members of my Christian writers groups: *Word Weavers*, and *Scribes*.

I am grateful for the Christian dream authors from the 1960s who paved the way for the rest of us. For insight that deeply influenced my journey into the hidden realm of dreams, special thanks to my friends, Catholic lay evangelists, Ralph and Pauline Nault; Baptist minister, the late Rev. Herman Riffel; and the late Dr. Bruce Morgan.

Above all, I thank God, who has graced me with divine nighttime communications that have profoundly impacted my life.

Introduction

My friend, the late Rev. Herman Riffel, said, "The dream is the voice of God[a] speaking to us in the night while our conscious mind is stilled."[7] As our intellect sleeps, our Creator speaks to us in another part of us, to our heart. Because of this, dreams can bring us into contact with the living God in a way we might not otherwise experience.

A dream is like a living word from God, alive and active—not a static, encrypted message. Since dreams contain divine energy, they can impact us deeply in every dimension of our lives. Dreams are able to penetrate our heart and impart life to us—inspiring, empowering, motivating, healing, or transforming us in some way.

In the Christian approach to dreams, we start with the belief that God wants to communicate with us. This is the cornerstone of why we value our dreams and work with them. Far more than just handing us advice or prophetic revelations, the dream helps us develop more awareness of the immediacy of our Lord, the very Source of our lives.

As a spiritual practice, working with dreams can take on a sacredness, facilitating a closer relationship with our God.

The voice of God in dreams

The Bible relates many stories of people who experienced God personally. Often we read that the *Word of the Lord* came to so-and-so.[b] How did this living Word come? Dr. Morton Kelsey[c] says he knows, "no better way

---

a When I refer to "hearing the voice of God," I am not talking about a literal, audible voice. I mean being aware in our spiritual senses—through visions, dreams, prophetic inspiration, intuitive knowing, and spiritual thoughts—that God is communicating with us.

b In the writings of the Old Testament prophets, picture-based *visions* are described as God's *Word* (Isa 2:1, 13:1; Jer 1:11; Mic 1:1; Ezek 1:1-3; Zech 1:7-8; Amos 7:1,4,7; 8:10).

c The late Episcopalian priest, counselor, and university professor, Morton Kelsey (1917-2001), authored more than 30 books, including *Dreams, A Way To Hear God*, and *God, Dreams, And Revelation: A Christian Interpretation Of Dreams*.

to achieve this experience … than through the dream."[8] Many men and women in the Bible, and throughout history, have been approached by God through dreams.

In Genesis 15:1-21, the Lord God appeared to Abraham in a vision/dream, conversing with him about his future. The Lord also conversed with Solomon in a dream, asking him what he wished God would give him (1 Kgs 3:5-15). In another interesting incident, God spoke directly to Abimelech (a heathen) in a dream about Abraham's wife Sarah (Gen 20:1-8).

Although these stories concern God speaking directly with His people, most dreams are indirect communication from our Creator, using word pictures. Hearing from God about his destiny, Joseph dreamed that his sheaf stood erect while his brothers' sheaves bowed to his (Gen 37:5-8). A Midianite soldier (another unbeliever) dreamed of a bread loaf tumbling into camp. A fellow soldier immediately understood its message: God has given the camp of Midian into the hand of Gideon (Judg 7:13-15).

Dream language

Most dreams convey their messages indirectly using pictures and images in a figurative and imaginative way—through word pictures. This is the language Jesus employed to convey His spiritual truths. By using symbolic language, Jesus showed us that effective communication often requires skirting around the conscious mind to engage the heart directly.

We must learn how to open up our symbolic dream communications for their meaning to be revealed to us. This requires some effort on our part. The Hebrew words for *interpretation* suggest that a dream must be cracked open to understand its obscure message (Judg 7:15, Gen 40:8).

What Is Christian Dream Work?

I choose to use the term *dream work*, rather than *dream interpretation* in my seminars and books. The idea of "dream work" allows us to move away from reliance upon professional interpreters to tell us what our dream means. Christian dream work empowers us to relate to our own dream and, with reliance upon the Holy Spirit, understand its message.

Although God can use spiritually-attuned men and women to help us draw out the meaning of a dream, *the Holy Spirit is central in our approach to unlocking the mystery of our dreams.*

An emphasis on dream work, rather than dream interpretation, offers more ways to approach our dreams, including meditative and imaginative strategies. It puts us in touch with resources other than our ego. Going beyond merely analytical exploration, dream work facilitates our relationship with God. When we work with a dream, it is important to be aware that we may be encountering the living God.

According to David Benner,[d] dreams invite us to engage them; they are not just passive communications that simply present information.[9] In dream work we focus on a particular dream, giving it an intentional response. Selecting from a variety of approaches, we relate to the dream, interact with its symbolic images, and make felt connections to its basic point or purpose.

It's art, not science

I prefer to think of Christian dream work as more an art, not a science. Since most dreams can't be opened up rationally, we must engage them by using our intuition and imagination. That's likely to be more productive than using reason and logic to try to understand a symbolic dream intellectually.

With this approach we enter into a kind of dialogue with God that allows the images spontaneously to spring alive with meaning for our lives. As our heart is touched, an "*Aha!*" may bring a sudden quickening, a *knowing*, that releases an emotional overflow—we cry, laugh, or feel bodily tension release.

Stay flexible

I recommend not relying on any single philosophical or theoretical perspective. There is no single strategy or technique for a particular dream that conveys the richness of dream work. A tenet of dream work is that we each have our own dream "language." In other words, any particular dream element[e] can differ in its meaning from person to person. We must not rely on a cookbook approach.

All dreams are not equally significant. Some are far more important than others and often have powerful emotions connected to them. Feel-

---

d Dr. David G. Benner (1947-) is an internationally known Christian psychologist, author, and lecturer who has authored numerous books on Christian spirituality, transformation, and soul care. http://www.drdavidgbenner.ca/ http://en.wikipedia.org/wiki/David_G._Benner.

e Element refers to any distinguishable feature in a dream: people, objects, places, weather, buildings, animals, sensations, emotions, etc.

ings that stay with us after we awaken are indicative of a very significant dream. See #10 *Biblical Purposes*; #11 *How Important Is This Dream?*; and #20 *Dream Intensity* to learn about different types of dreams and how to recognize more important ones.

Dreams carry divine purpose

Dreams contain divine purpose, offering us help for every dimension of our lives. They often show us the thoughts and intentions of our hearts, prepare us for what's ahead, or focus our attention on something we need to consider. Dreams are loaded with truths. They come to show us something we need to see; they never come to judge or condemn us.

Jesus promised that we would know the truth, and the truth would set us free. This is why the Holy Spirit, the Spirit of truth, is vital in our spiritual journey. King David understood this when he prayed: "You desire truth in the innermost being, and in the hidden part [the unseen part] You will make me know wisdom" (Ps 51:6).

We desperately need truth in our inner most being, so we can break free from the destructive lies of the kingdom of darkness. This is one reason why dreams are helpful in our journey to wholeness.

Dreams, the language of the Holy Spirit

In the Old Testament, God promised He would pour out His Spirit and make His words known to us (Prov 1:23). The prophet Joel tells us that a time will come when the Holy Spirit is poured forth, and ordinary people will receive dreams, visions, and prophecies (Joel 2:28).

At Pentecost it happened. St. Peter reminds them that the coming of the Holy Spirit will result in God speaking through prophecies, visions, and dreams (Acts 2:16-18).

Dream Work, A Search For Hidden Treasure

Christian dream work is based on a spiritual worldview, acknowledging the existence of an inner spiritual realm which can be known to us directly, through the eyes of the heart.[10] According to the findings of research, dreams originate from an unconscious (unseen) area within us, enabling us to experience the spiritual realm that is difficult to contact any other way.

Central to a Christian approach to dreams is the belief that we contain a vast unconscious life—the inner world where our rational mind cannot go—which is a storehouse of hidden wealth deposited by God. Church Father, Synesius of Cyrene,*f* found dreams to be an almost inexhaustible source of riches.[11] Centuries later, psychiatrist M. Scott Peck wrote that dreams are a manifestation of grace, revealing the existence of a concealed domain inside us that "contains riches beyond imagination."[12]

In other words, we have secret, hidden riches deposited by God within us (2 Cor 4:7; Col 2:3). Because it's buried beyond the reach of our conscious minds, we need to learn how to draw it out. That's what dream work is all about—the art of drawing out the divine guidance, counsel, and instruction contained in the dream. It is about the search for great treasure buried in the field of our souls.

Avoid these pitfalls

As with any other attempt to understand the supernatural realm, we must learn to discern what is or isn't from God. We should reject any teaching on dreams that does not follow biblical guidelines. Christian authors on dreams concur that any interpretation contradicting principles in the Holy Scriptures is not valid.

Christian dream work requires that we discern and test our interpretations properly. In #32 *Test Your Interpretation*, I suggest some biblical guidelines and principles to help you avoid the risks of misinterpretation. Because you'll be working with a somewhat unfamiliar language, you need to be aware of common mistakes we can make.

Some errors I see frequently:

1. Taking dreams literally, when they are symbolic.
2. Making the dream be about the other person in it, not our self.
3. Projecting our wishes and desires into our dreams.
4. Feeling embarrassed by our dream images.
5. Trusting our intellectual reasoning, not our spiritual senses.
6. Relying on a cookbook approach to unlock the meaning of symbolic images.
7. Accepting someone's interpretation of our dream without our heart's agreement.

---

f Early Orthodox Church Father and Bishop of Ptolemais, Synesius of Cyrene (c. 373-414), found dreams to be a tremendous source of riches. His highly regarded book, *On Dreams,* is one of the most scholarly discussions of dreams until the 20th century.

8. Making major life decisions based on a dream, without further confirmation from God.

9. Using dreams as fortune-telling tools, relating to dreams only as prophetic revelations.

10. Using dreams to control or manipulate others.

11. Fear of Satan giving us dreams. (In nearly every discussion of dreams, someone asks whether Satan can give us dreams. In my experience, I have not heard of a dream that seemed to have its origins in Satan. To the contrary, I have found that troubling dreams of demonic spirits or satanic involvement were given by God. He brought the dreams to warn, show how to pray, reveal the truth about something, or prepare dreamers for situations they might meet in their families, personal lives, or ministry.)

Twenty reasons why we work with dreams:

1. Impart spiritual blessings.

2. Establish promises from God.

3. Edify us and build us up.

4. Give us creative, inspired ideas.

5. Reveal our gifts, potential, calling, and anointing.

6. Provide clear instruction about actions we need to take.

7. Give us guidance and direction; warn us about wrong decisions.

8. Offer insight into problems we are currently struggling with.

9. Reveal things God has for us to do and when to do them.

10. Nurture our physical, psychological, and spiritual well-being.

11. Reveal truth about ourselves, our blind spots, destructive attitudes or behaviors.

12. Help us see our weaknesses and acknowledge our failures.

13. Enable us to connect to our feelings, or release pent-up emotions.

14. Open us to spiritual reality, bring us spiritual revelation.

15. Encourage us on our journey to wholeness and freedom.

16. Touch us with God's love, peace, or comfort.

17. Impart to us divine energy and faith.

18. Reveal direct attack of demonic spirits on us or others.

19. Show us how to pray.

20. Bring us God's answer to our prayers.

Trust the Holy Spirit

Although Jesus Christ talked about hiding things in parables, He also said the kingdom treasures are available to those who earnestly seek and knock. Our natural mind is inadequate, but our spiritual mind can understand the things of the Spirit of God. The Holy Spirit knows the meaning of every dream and the best way for us to benefit from it.

We study, we learn, we meditate, we pray, but our spiritual growth and transformation depend on God revealing to us what He wants us to know—the Holy Spirit is vital for discernment.

With God's help, we can approach our dreams with confidence. As we work with our dream, we thank God for this gift, and then put all of its content and all of our tools and techniques into His hands. We can trust the Holy Spirit to help us understand our dreams.

Be blessed in opening your letters from God,

Judith Doctor

Dear Dreamer,

I call you Dreamer because I know everyone dreams. Research scientists, whether they believe in me or not, affirm that you dream every night. I can't believe (and belief and faith are my specialties) you don't value your dreams in the 21st century!

People have been discovering hidden treasure in their dreams since the dawn of creation (well, just after Adam started breathing, anyway). Through dreams I bring people encouragement, instruction, ideas, warnings, guidance, counsel, wisdom, you name it.

In dreams throughout the Old Testament, I spoke to Abraham, I spoke to Isaac, I spoke to Jacob, I spoke to Joseph, I spoke to hundreds of my prophets. Nobody doubted it was my Word coming to them visually during the night hours. They accepted my Word and acted on it, as well they should.

Same thing in the New Testament. Joseph, Mary, Paul, even the wife of that rascal, Pompous Pilate, heard from me in dreams. I have continually been communicating with my creation through dreams and visions. Always did. Still do.

Now what's going on in my world in this era that people in the church are ignoring the dreams that I am bringing them every night? Some time in the near future I want to hear your side of this: why do you reject this awesome means to hear from me while you sleep?

Tell you what: I'm going to redouble my efforts. Expect more dreams, more vivid dreams, ones you'll remember. The Holy Spirit will be right there with you to help you understand the bizarre images I prefer to send to help get you out of your ordinary thinking.

Lovingly,

Your Heavenly Father

Part One

Fundamental Skills

In Part One, I introduce you to seven fundamental skills and practices essential to the art of Christian dream work. You will learn foundational dream work principles that will start you on the right path.

Dream work principles

☆ Dreams have a divine author.

☆ God promises to speak through dreams in the night.

☆ Keeping a dream journal is a spiritual practice.

☆ Most dreams speak about the things important to our heart.

☆ Dream work techniques enable us to dynamically interact with our dreams.

☆ Correct interpretation brings an *"Aha!"* moment.

☆ Christian dream work relies on prayer, faith, and humility.

Dear Pharaoh,

You have found favor with me because you're a man who listens to his dreams. This is essential if you are going to keep track of what's happening and to know how to live your life successfully. Since you are responsible for a lot of people in your kingdom, you need to pay close attention to the next dream you experience—it has far reaching importance for all of Egypt.

In fact, when you understand this dream (and another one I have planned for you—stay on the alert), it will rock your entire world. Here's how it goes:

Pharaoh stood by the river. Suddenly out of the river came seven fine looking fat cows. Then seven ugly and gaunt cows came out of the river and ate up the seven fine looking fat cows. (taken from Genesis 41:1-4)

Respectfully,

Yahweh, God of Joseph and the Israelis

1

Take Dreams Seriously

" ... in the last days," God says, "... I will pour forth of My Spirit upon all mankind; And your sons and your daughters shall prophesy, and your young men shall see visions, and your old men shall dream dreams." – Acts 2:17

The dream *has a Divine author!*[13] It is not simply, as many of us were taught, a pointless process of experiencing stimuli from our senses while we sleep. I have discovered that God is the source behind our dreams—as emphasized at Pentecost.

Dreams, a gift from God

Early in the 3rd century, the great apologist, *Tertullian,*[a] affirmed this truth when he said, "Dreams are one of the gifts from God, a charisma, and this gift was not restricted to the ancients in the Bible, but was equally promised to us."[14] Church Father, Ambrose,[b] taught that dreams were one of God's methods for bringing revelation to man.

If we believe dreams are a gift from God and that He wants to speak to us through them, we will begin to pay sincere attention to them. We'll clearly decide that we want God's help and direction for our life, and we will give our dreams serious consideration. The late Episcopalian priest, Dr. Morton Kelsey, wrote:

> Our attitude toward dreams, which are as delicate, complex, and alive as human beings, is of paramount importance. When we do take our dreams seriously, we discover that they have some powerful and transforming messages for us.[15]

---

a Christian Apologist, Tertullian (c.160-225), was called the "Creator of Christian Latin literature." He summarizes his theory of dreams and their relation to the Christian doctrine of revelation in his major work, *A Treatise of the Soul.*

b Ambrose (c.340–397), Church Doctor in the West and Archbishop of Milan, valued his dreams, even going to confront the emperor because of a dream.

Wake up call

My wake up call to dreams came seven years into my spiritual journey. When I awoke in the morning, I recalled snippets of dreams—a young doe shot by a hunter, a porpoise breaking the surface of the ocean, a one-eyed pelican on the ocean floor. Why these images? What do they mean? I wondered if they were from God. If so, what was He trying to say to me through them? Could I trust them? So I asked God to show me His truth about dreams.

Shortly after my prayer, I dreamed the following: I'm looking at a file cabinet with a drawer pulled wide open. I see three folders. The first is labeled "Guidance from the dream," the second, "Guidance from the shadow," and the third ... well, I just couldn't remember it. I awoke knowing that my dreams were from God! He'd answered my prayer in the night. Right then, I made a decision to trust that God was speaking to me through my dreams, giving me His wise counsel, guidance, and direction for my life.

In the past thirty-three years, I have not been disappointed. Because of my dreams, my life has been far richer than I ever dreamed possible, and my relationship with God became deeper. Unlocking the mystery of my dreams has created opportunities for inner healing and psychological and spiritual growth. Now I understand this Scripture: "I will give you the *treasures* of darkness, and hidden wealth of secret places, in order that you may know that it is I, the Lord" (Isa 45:3).

Attend to and respect our dreams

Nothing of great value comes easily. The more attention and respect we give our dreams, the more we receive back from them. Gold and diamonds having the greatest value lie deepest in the earth. To mine the field of your dreams for the hidden wisdom of God, you must want it with all your heart.

Dr. Morton Kelsey said he launched his serious study of dreams because of his own troubling dreams. He admitted having "an intellectual faith but little experiential knowledge of the Divine." His dreams revealed his anxieties and indicated how to resolve his issues, enabling him to experience "the presence of a loving, caring God."[16]

1. Cultivate dreams

Here are some ideas to help prepare you to remember your dreams.

- Resolve in your heart that you want to pay attention to your dreams.
- Don't set an alarm—at least on weekends. Alarms shatter dream recall.
- Do something to shift your thoughts to a more reflective posture, perhaps by listening to soft, contemplative music—anything that promotes a peaceful, reflective atmosphere.
- Carry out a meaningful custom that you choose to associate with dreaming, such as meditating on a Scripture, song, or religious painting.
- Read a parable by Jesus, allowing yourself to get in touch with its word pictures.
- Before falling asleep try saying, "Speak Lord, I am listening."

2. Ask God a question before sleeping

Church Father, Synesius of Cyrene,[c] suggested people who want to hear from God through dreams should pray for them.[17] He observed that by cultivating dreams, not only do we gain practical results, but we also experience great joy from the sense of communication with God.

- Ask God to speak to you through your dreams.
- Before going to sleep, think of a problem you need God's help with.
- State the problem as a specific question; perhaps write it in your journal.
- Pray, asking God for an answer.

---

c Early Orthodox Church Father and Bishop of Ptolemais, Synesius of Cyrene (c. 373-414), found dreams to be a tremendous source of riches. His highly regarded book, *On Dreams*, is one of the most scholarly discussions of dreams until the 20th century.

▤ Ancient dreamer—King Abimelech

King Abimelech (c. 2050 BC), a Philistine King, had taken Abraham's wife because he thought she was Abraham's sister. But God came to Abimelech in a dream of the night and said, "Behold, you are a dead man because of the woman whom you have taken, for she is married."

But Abimelech had not come near her, and he said, "Lord, will You slay a nation, even though blameless? Did he not say, 'She is my sister'? And she said, 'He is my brother.' In the integrity of my heart and the innocence of my hands I have done this."

Then God said to him in the dream, "Yes, I know that ... and I also kept you from sinning against Me; therefore I did not let you touch her. Now therefore, restore the man's wife, for he is a prophet, and he will pray for you, and you will live."

Abimelech arose early in the morning, and called all his servants and told all these things in their hearing; and the men were greatly frightened. (Gen 20:2-18)

2

God, Did You Speak
To Me During The Night?

Indeed God speaks once, or twice, yet no one notices it. In a dream, in a vision of the night ... while they slumber in their beds, then He opens the ears of men and seals their instruction. – Job 33:14-16

When I first awaken in the morning, I like to ask God if He communicated with me during the night. The Bible tells us that *God will speak to us in a dream or vision of the night*, while we are sound asleep. I don't fully understand how God gives us dreams, but I have experienced them firsthand again and again. Here is how Clement of Alexandria[d] explained it: "During sleep we are especially open to spiritual reality because our soul is not bothered by sense input as it is during waking hours."[18]

Keep watch to see what God will say

We can cultivate the habit of asking the Lord if He spoke to us during the night in a dream, and to bring it to our memory. Here's a suggested approach: As you come out of your sleep, don't allow yourself to become fully alert, don't open your eyes, don't even move. While lingering in the twilight zone between night and day, reflect back over the night to see if a dream or a thought from God floats into your consciousness—perhaps keeping watch like Habakkuk did:

I will keep watch to see what He will speak to me ... Then the Lord answered me and said, 'Record the vision and inscribe it on tablets, that the one who reads it may run' (Hab 2:1-2).

If a dream surfaces, thank the Lord for it, then immediately record it. If you can't get up during the night, repeat it to yourself a few times before going back to sleep—this helps shift the dream into the memory

---

d Christian Apologist and Church Father, Clement of Alexandria (c. 150–215), was an educated
   man familiar with classical Greek.

part of your brain. If you are unable to recall any dreams, try noting the mood or feelings you have when you awaken. These are often the result of dreams.

Sharing dreams at breakfast

If you are not able to log or record your dream immediately, tell it to someone as soon as you can. Over morning coffee, my husband, Gerald, and I often ask each other, *Did you have a dream last night?* Frequently, this seems to prompt recall of a dream that we'd let drift away.

One morning in 1979, I recalled the following dream at breakfast with friends:[e] I am admiring some new floral slipcovers a woman had made for her old sofa. The fabric motif is a large leafy pattern. As I shared my dream, my friend responded, "Fig leaves. They are fig leaves!" I knew he was right. Like the Pharisees, I was concerned with the outside appearance of the cup, but not allowing God to clean me on the inside (see Matt 23:25).

1. Ask the Lord if He spoke to you during the night

- When you awaken, wait to see if God spoke to you while you slept.
- If you cannot remember a dream, note your mood or feeling as you awaken.

2. Not dreaming?

King Nebuchadnezzar also may have had this problem (Dan 2). Perhaps we ignore our dreams because some inner voice tells us they are not important.[19] We are steeped in a Western worldview that denies the validity of dreams and makes us fear and distrust them. It's easy to understand why we disregard our dreams. Try giving yourself permission to dream before going to sleep.

Or perhaps you may need to pray, "Lord, I ask you to forgive me for being afraid of listening to my dreams. Please remove any barrier that keeps me from recalling my dreams." Use your journal to explore why you don't remember your dreams. Write the following questions, then listen inside, and write the thoughts coming to you spontaneously.

---

[e] Ralph & Pauline Nault. Since Ralph closed his electrical contracting business in the 1970s, he and Pauline have ministered as Catholic lay evangelists (http://www.thenewlife.us/). See Ralph's blog: (http://www.ralphnault.com/blog/).

- "Lord, why am I unable to remember my dreams?"
- Is there a problem, an obstacle, or a challenge I am refusing to face?
- Am I holding back from dreams because of something I am afraid to look at?

⊡ 19th c. dreamer— Thérèse of Lisieux

St. Thérèse of Lisieux (1873-1897), a year before her death at age 24, wrote that her worthless soul was very storm-tossed. Then she added, "I remember thinking about the wonderful dreams which certain souls have been privileged to experience, and how consoling an experience it would be; but I didn't pray for anything of the kind. I thought that dreams weren't for unimportant souls like mine."

In the early morning hours the next day, she dreamed: "I was aware of three Carmelite sisters in their mantles and big veils. One sister moved towards me and lifted her veil and threw it over me … It was Mother Anne … I asked her, 'Tell me whether God means to leave me much longer on earth? Or will He come to fetch me soon?' Mother Anne replied, 'Yes, soon; very soon, I promise you.'

Then I asked: 'Does God really ask no more of me than these unimportant little sacrifices I offer him, these desires to do something better?' She answered, 'God asks no more. He is content with you.'"

When she awoke her inner storm no longer raged, and she was filled with joy and contentment with her life. She wrote, "Jesus, my Beloved, this was only a prelude to greater graces still with which You'd determine to enrich me … ." She continually recalled the dream with delight for the next several months before her death.[20]

3

Record Your Dream

Daniel saw a dream and visions in his mind as he lay on his bed; then he wrote the dream down and related the following summary [words] of it. – Daniel 7:1

O nce you wake up, you have only a few minutes to grab hold of that dream. If you don't capture the dream right away, it's gone (researchers say 95% are lost after five minutes). Write it on paper, speak it into a recorder, key it into an electronic device—whatever way you choose, get it down without delay.

In recording your dream, do it quickly, using a first-person narrative style, without correcting your grammar or punctuation. Even if only a small fragment floats into your consciousness, latch onto it. More pieces will probably come as you write.

Don't try to evaluate the dream, understand its meaning or interpret it as you are writing. Simply writing it down will make it grow more vivid and help you to remember more details. It's kind of like fishing—just pull on the line and see what you reel in.

When you don't have time to write a full description of the dream, just quickly log its highlights. Or, even if you're not artistically inclined, you may like to draw a rough sketch of the dream in your journal. Go back later and fill in the details.

When you finish recording your dream, take a few minutes simply to think about it, to just *feel* it. This brief attention honors both the dream and the Giver of the dream. It also allows time for additional details or meaning to come to mind.

Sometimes you may have an immediate sense of what God is trying to show you through the dream. At other times, you will want to draw out the inner meaning of its symbolic images by using various dream work ideas, strategies, and techniques described in this book.

Dream journaling started in biblical times

Writing down or telling dreams is not new. People in the Bible and in the early church wrote down what God told them, often recounting it to others. Daniel gives the biblical precedent for recording dreams and telling them to others. Maintaining the biblical tradition, Church Father, Synesius of Cyrene, recommended keeping a dream journal as a way to "publish our waking and sleeping visions and their attendant circumstances."[21]

Wonderful things happen when we commit our dreams to writing. This is the act that transforms our dream into something more. Your dream record provides the basis for further reflection, dream work, and future insight. With it you can preserve the ongoing story of your dream life and build your own dream dictionary.

Dream work, a spiritual practice

Consider your dream journal as a spiritual practice, enabling you to keep a record of the things God speaks to you personally in the night. Recording your dreams will help you make connections between events in your outer conscious world and those occurring in your dream world.

Even if you never work with your dream again, the act of writing it down is significant. It lets God know that you're listening. It also signals the Lord that you are taking the dream seriously.

Dreams as story

Throughout history, Christians have developed their dream/vision experiences into story form. Apostolic Father, Hermas,[f] a former slave, used his own visions and dreams to write *The Shepherd of Hermas*.[22] In the fourth century, Church Doctor, Gregory of Nazianzen, wrote theological poems based on his own dream experiences.[23]

In more modern times, John Bunyan[g] wrote *Pilgrim's Progress* from a series of his own dreams, visions, and contemplative experiences. His book—one of the most popular books for several hundred years—is actually the story of his inner life, of his conversion and spiritual journey.

---

f *The Shepherd of Hermas* is an inspirational Christian allegory that is based on several dream/ visions Hermas experienced. Considered as canonical Scripture by many 2nd & 3rd century Christians, the book was read for three centuries in several languages.

g John Bunyan (1628-1688) was an English Christian writer and preacher who wrote his renowned book, *Pilgrim's Progress*, while imprisoned for preaching the gospel.

Collecting dream stories

Stored away in boxes, I have volumes of journals recorded over many years. I am reluctant to toss them out because they contain precious dreams through which God gave me spiritual revelation, and guidance and direction for my life—my personal story.

Here is a dream I logged in my journal many years ago: While I am sitting in a Christian meeting, an offering basket is being passed. A voice says to me, "Give Me something from your purse." I look in my purse and see only a needle & thread and a magnifying lens. I put them in the offering basket.

When I awoke, I immediately knew that it was God who was speaking to me. I pondered the dream images. Why a needle & thread? A magnifying lens? It was obvious: God was telling me that He didn't want me to try to mend a certain situation, neither did He want me to focus on it, making it bigger. I was to surrender the situation to Him, by putting my efforts in the offering basket.

1. Start a dream journal

- Choose something special—notebook, dream journal, electronic recorder—to record your dreams.
- Place your journal or recorder near your bed as an act of faith.
- Record your dream as soon as you awaken.

2. Record your dream

- Establish a dedicated place to sit while you record your dream.
- Date your dream entry.
- Write a detailed description of your dream, without analyzing or interpreting it.
- Try writing in present tense instead of past tense.
- Note all elements in your dream. Dream elements refer to all distinguishable features. (For a list of elements see #27 *Identify Dream Elements*.)

3. Record your immediate Reaction (R)

After recording your dream, describe your immediate Reaction (R) to it—your spontaneous impressions, thoughts, and feelings upon awakening. These might offer clues to the area of your life it is about, or to its meaning.

- How did the dream affect you as you awoke? Exhausted? Invigorated? Contented? Peaceful? Unprepared? Depressed? Comforted?
- What feelings were still present in you? Sadness? Excitement? Disappointment? Joy? Confusion? Pleasure? Frustration? Anxiety?
- Did the dream immediately bring something to mind: thoughts, memories, recollections, associations?
- Have you seen any of the dream images recently in your waking life?

4. Dream journal format

You can develop your own format for recording dreams. Using a consistent format will make it easier in the future to go back and find things. As you record, be sure to include the following items:

- Date: write the date in the same place.
- Dream description: write down everything you can remember about the dream.
- (R): your immediate Reaction and thoughts upon awakening.

▣ 16th c. dreamer— Elector Frederick the Wise

On the morning of October 31, 1517 (just before Luther nailed his 95 theses to the door of Wittenberg Castle church), Elector Frederick the Wise reported a dream to Duke John. Frederick said it was so deeply impressed upon his mind that he would not forget it if he lived a thousand years. The dream was repeated three times, each with new circumstances.

I dreamed that Almighty God sent me a monk, who asked permission to write on the Wittenberg Castle church door. The monk wrote in such large characters that I could read the writing at Schweinitz. His pen was so large its end reached Rome, where it pierced the ears of a lion crouching there, and shook the triple crown on the Pope's head.

All the cardinals and princes tried to prevent it from falling. I awoke, enraged at the monk for not managing his pen better. I fell asleep, and the dream returned. The lion, still annoyed by the pen, began to roar loudly. The whole city of Rome, and all the States of the Holy Empire, ran to see what the matter was.

I again awoke, repeated the Lord's Prayer and once more fell asleep. I dreamed that all the princes of the Empire tried to break the pen, but it seemed to be made of iron. The monk said the pen belonged to an old Bohemian goose. Suddenly I heard a loud noise—a large number of other pens had sprung out of the monk's pen.[24]

4

Identify Current Concerns

*I will bless the Lord who has counseled me; Indeed, my mind [lit. inner man]
instructs me in the night. – Psalm 16:7*

Most dreams seem to come in the immediate context of our lives, our
current issues and recent life experiences—conflicts, problems; accidents, traumas, illnesses; crises, troubling situations; prayers; decisions
we need to make. In dream work, we call these issues our Current Concerns (CC).

Most dreams are about the concerns on our heart

Research shows that dreams are speaking to us about the concerns on our
heart and the factors influencing them. Dream researcher Calvin Hall
found that most dreams are about everyday concerns—not repressed or
hidden conflicts.[25] This is a fundamental principle of Christian dream
work: *most dreams speak about the things important to your own heart.*

Identifying your current concerns and relating them to your dream is
key to unlocking the messages from God contained in it. If you don't take
time to immediately note them, you will probably not be able to recall
them later.

Often people come to me for help with a dream that they received
perhaps many weeks, months, or even years ago. But it is difficult to help
them, because they draw a blank when I ask them about what was going
on in their lives at the time of the dream. Most dreams are coming to help
us with the things on our heart at that time.

In 1985, after seeing changes in me, a close friend asked me to start
a small group, teaching others what I had learned. I'd never led a small
group before. *Could I do it?*, I wondered. Then I dreamed: I am sitting in
a small circle of people. A woman leading the group looks over at me and
says, "Skilled talent."

As I awoke, faith quickened in my heart. I could do this! God has
gifted me with the talent to facilitate small groups. Soon after, I started

my first small group, helping others experience, as I had, spiritual growth and transformation through the Holy Spirit.

Pay attention to dreams when seeking God on an issue

We need to be especially alert to our dreams, if we are seeking God on an issue. When Saul's enemies were gathered against him, he expected God to answer in the usual ways: Urim, prophets, or dreams. Similarly, when we seek the Lord, we can expect Him to answer—sometimes in our dreams (I Sam 28:6,15).

Here is an example from the life of an early Christian, St. Perpetua.[h] Imprisoned in Carthage, Perpetual asked God to give her a dream revealing her fate. God answered her in a dream: She saw a dragon at the foot of a golden ladder stretching upward toward the heavens. Daggers and hooks attached to the ladder slashed anyone who failed to keep looking up. She and her fellow prisoners climbed on the ladder. When she awoke, she understood they would die.[26]

Pay attention to dreams at certain times

We must be particularly alert to dreams at certain times in our life—marriage, divorce, graduation, job change, major illness or crisis, recent trauma, birthday, anniversary, holiday, and religious celebrations.

Other times to be especially attentive: when we are involved in spiritual mentoring or counseling, or when we are being extraordinarily intentional in seeking God about something.

1. Identify your Current Concerns (CC)

Stop and reflect on what was going on the day or two before your dream. To help you identify your Current Concerns (CC), ask the following questions:

- What concerns or questions has my heart been struggling with?
- What issues do I need to resolve? What decisions do I need to make?
- What significant events are happening?
- What problems do I need God's help with?
- What prayers have I been praying?

---

[h] St. Perpetua (c. 181–202), along with her slave, Felicity, was martyred at Carthage in the Roman province of Africa.

- What was I thinking about when I went to bed? Was I upset or worried about anything?
- Did I go to sleep with any leftover feelings from my day?

2. Log your Current Concerns (CC)

After recording your dream and immediate Reaction (R), log your Current Concerns (CC), just something to trigger your memory later.

3. Connect your Current Concerns (CC) to your dream

Now look to see how the dream might be reflecting your current concerns.

- What comment does my dream make about how I am handling situations in life?
- Does the description fit a circumstance in my waking life?
- What metaphorical comment might it be making about my inner life?

▣ 20ᵗʰ c. dreamer— *Shayda, a former Muslim*

Shayda,* who came from a militant Islamic background, was married to a man who had formerly been associated with Hezbollah. Now a Christian, he urged her to attend a women's Bible study group. When she heard the women talking about God speaking to them, in her heart she mocked them, *God never answers my prayer. He doesn't speak to women.* She cried out to God, "Talk to me, if You are there." That night she dreamed this dream:

I am under a beautiful blue sky, walking through tall green grass with three other women and Jesus. Suddenly Jesus and two of the women are far ahead, with a cliff and valley separating us. Jesus calls to me, "Come, my daughter, do not be afraid." But I answer, "It is a valley, master." When He repeats, "Do not be afraid," I and the other woman step out, holding hands like innocent children. We walk forward on level, beautiful ground.

In the morning, she awoke feeling very happy, and excitedly told her husband that Jesus had talked to her in her dream. At the next women's meeting, Shayda also had something to share: God speaks to her, too.[27]

---

* A few years ago, Shayda (not her real name) and her husband were visiting with our friends and shared this dream with them.

5

The TTAQ Technique

King Solomon said that "counsel in the heart of man is like deep water, but a man of understanding will draw it out." – Proverbs 20:5 (KJV)

The TTAQ (Title, Theme, Affect, Question) is an easy-to-use, four-step dream work technique.[28] These simple steps will focus your attention on the information already present in the dream, and enable *you* to dynamically interact with it. I have discovered that, if all you do is use this technique, you will gain significant insight into what God is trying to show you—and you might encounter the living God.

Let's learn from King Solomon. This wisest of all men—himself a famous dreamer—says that buried very deep within our heart is some type of helpful advice. In order to access this divine advice, it must be brought up into our awareness, like a bucket draws up water from a well. He warns, however, that it requires *understanding*—the capacity to separate, distinguish, and discern—to discover the treasure in the bucket.

1. Title (T)—give dream a title

A simple dream work practice is to give the dream a Title (T). In addition to helping you identify the dream in your journal, titling the dream can give you a key to unraveling its meaning. Following are some ideas to help you title your dream:

- If there is a specific message or key statement in the dream, turn this into your title.
- Choose a title capturing the most unusual element of the dream.
- Pretend you're an artist and you want to title your freshly hung painting.
- Imagine you just wrote a short story that needs a title.
- Try asking the dream, by what name or title it wishes to be addressed.
- Write the Title (T) at the top of your dream entry.

2. Theme (T)—determine basic theme

The Theme (T) refers to the major issue, conflict, or problem set up by the dream—trying to find your way, climb a hill, perform a task, contact someone, take a test; losing a child, a purse; missing a bus or train or plane; discovering a new room.

For a particularly complex dream, identify the main issue in each scene. If several themes are involved, note them all, then prioritize the most important ones. Determine if one theme or motif dominates the dream. If you have difficulty determining a theme, use questions like these to help you:

- What is this dream mainly about?
- What is the key issue or problem the dream addresses?
- State the basic Theme (T) in one sentence.

3. Affect (A)—identify primary affect

Next, determine the Affect (A) present in the dream. Affect refers to the primary emotion or basic feeling expressed in the dream. This step seems to be the most difficult for some dreamers. Not familiar with their own emotions, they often lack the vocabulary to identify the emotions in their dreams.

If you have trouble finding the emotion, try imagining what you might have felt. Or ask someone else to help you. Ask, "If this were your dream, what might you be feeling in it?"

- Identify the emotions or feelings expressed in the dream.
- What did *you* feel about what was happening in the dream?
- Record the primary emotion or dominant feeling, Affect (A).

4. Question (Q)—determine question dream is asking

Rather than expecting dreams to give answers, advice, or prophetic revelation, some authors suggest we view dreams as bringing us a Question (Q).[29] Approaching the dream this way shifts our focus away from us and directs our attention toward God. We then begin to relate to the Source of our dream.

- "Lord, what question are you asking me in this dream?"
- What is my dream asking me? What does it want from me?
- Select the most compelling Question (Q); log it in your journal.
- Reflect/meditate on the question, inviting the Lord to lead you.

▣ 18ᵗʰ c. dreamer— Dr. Benjamin Rush

Dr. Benjamin Rush (1745-1813), prominent physician and signer of the *Declaration of Independence*, was concerned about a long-standing feud between John Adams and Thomas Jefferson. Then he dreamed the following dream and shared it with his friend John Adams:

"What book is that in your hands?" said I to my son Richard.

"It is the history of the United States," said he. "Shall I read a page of it to you?"

"No, no," said I. "I believe in the truth of no history but in that which is contained in the Old & New Testaments."

"But, sir," said my son, "this page relates to your friend, Mr. Adams."

"Let me see it then."

Later, Rush sent a copy of his dream to John Adams, who replied, "My friend, there is something very serious in this business (of dreams). The Holy Ghost carries on the whole Christian system in this earth." ... As a result of Dr. Rush sharing his dream, John Adams and Thomas Jefferson were reconciled.[30]

Dream Journal Format: Here is how I log my dreams, including my immediate Reaction, Current Concerns & the TTAQ (see Chapters 3, 4 & 5).

T (Title): You've Got A Good Thing Going Here   March 23, 2006

A small group of women are staying in my house for a couple of days. They mill around my dining room, waiting to eat. The meat is on the table, and I am in the kitchen hurriedly trying to prepare the rest of the meal. They can't seem to wait any longer, and begin to pick at the meat hungrily. I tell them to wait, because "I am not ready yet."

Another small group arrives: they seem to be Europeans. Not expecting more guests, I am surprised, but I accept them. It is near evening time. I step out of the front door. An unknown man looks at me and says, "You've got a good thing going here." I nod in agreement, but I have a question, "Do I need official approval to have these guests in my home?"

R (Immediate Reaction): When I awoke, I felt excited. I sensed that the man on the steps was bringing me a message from God. The house reminds me of a lovely Victorian we redecorated and sold to a retired couple who turned it into a Bed & Breakfast.

CC (Current Concerns): I am at a pivotal point in my life, feeling unsure of what to do, now that I have my MSW degree. I have been asking the Lord to show me the direction to take, even though I don't feel ready for the next step. I have many questions. Also, the years in grad school have been rough, and I am concerned about my age and my stamina. Earlier, I had written in my journal, "Lord, I need a new vision for my life." I wondered if I needed to go through the hoops to become licensed as a social worker.

T (Theme): Trying to finish my meal preparation

A (Affect): Pressure, anxiety, concern

Q (Question): Are you willing to feed my sheep?

6

The "*Aha!*" Moment

For to us God revealed them through the Spirit ... Now we have received ... the Spirit who is from God, so that we may know the things freely given to us by God. – 1 Corinthians 2:10-12

In Christian dream work, we explore a dream to draw out its meaning and connect with God's divine purpose in it. When we have the correct interpretation, or come close to the meaning of the dream, something within us will leap in agreement. We refer to this as the "*Aha!*" moment, when the Holy Spirit witnesses to the truth of our discovery.

Because dream images are linked to energy deep within us, we may feel sparks fly when a connection is made. We might sense a shift in our mood that releases an overflow of emotions—laugh, cry, surprise—or perhaps a release of tension in our body. Some describe it as an inner click or intuitive knowing. Discovering something new, even negative, tends to bring a surge of energy, a flow of life within us.

We must stay alert to the still, small voice in our spirit, the thoughts that light spontaneously upon our mind, or the memories that float up to consciousness, without us digging for them. When we sense this witness of the Holy Spirit (the "*Aha!*"), we have unlocked the inner meaning of the dream and released its hidden treasure—God's wise counsel, instruction, and guidance for our life.

Making mistakes

We don't learn this in one easy lesson—it's a process. For example, a few years ago, we sensed we'd be moving; at first Gerald felt it was to Michigan. But when we learned a son and his family might be moving to Tucson, I dreamed the following: Gerald comes into the room and tells me that he just received a phone call, and we are moving to Tucson.

Instead of looking for an "*Aha!*" we made the mistake of taking *Tucson* literally. When our son and his family did not move there, I felt perplexed. As I prayed about my confusion, suddenly I understood the dream and experienced an "*Aha!*" that I recognized as the witness of the Holy Spirit. Employing a "sounds-like" pun, God was showing me that we would be moving near our two sons—who both lived in Michigan!

Spiritual senses

The Bible says that the natural mind cannot understand the things of the Spirit of God, but we can comprehend them through the Holy Spirit (1 Cor 2:9-16). St. Paul understood this when he prayed for the Christians at Ephesus, that "the eyes of their heart may be enlightened, that they may know ..." (Eph 1:18).

In the third century, Clement of Alexandria, encouraging us not to ignore the spiritual eyes, said ...

> Let us, not, then, who are sons of the true light, close the door against this light; but turning in on ourselves, illumining the eyes of the hidden man, and gazing on the truth itself ... [31]

As Christians, we have spiritual senses through which the Holy Spirit can witness to the truth of something—but we must learn to use them. You can trust the Holy Spirit.

1. Be aware of your spiritual senses
- Rely on the Holy Spirit to help you.
- Spiritual senses are key: if you do not use them, you can be misled with a wrong interpretation.
- If you are not aware of your spiritual senses, pray and ask the Lord to open them.

2. Be alert for the "Aha!"
- Learn to discern or recognize an "*Aha!*" moment within you.
- Do not rely on your excited emotions or analytical thoughts.
- Never accept an interpretation your heart doesn't respond to.

☑ 20th c. dreamer— Catherine Marshall LeSourd

Christian author Catherine Marshall LeSourd (1914-1983)* dreamed of a stinking head of a woman sitting on a pedestal in her living room. She understood that God was trying to show her that she relied too much on her intellect, instead of faith in her heart and the leading of the Holy Spirit.[32]

* Catherine (Marshall) LeSourd wrote many nonfiction, inspirational, and fiction works, including *A Man Called Peter; Christy; Beyond Ourselves; Something More;* and *The Helper.*

Approach Dream Work Prayerfully

C hristian dream work is not about divining the future, but about a way to listen to God. During the Dark Ages, the Western World lost sight of this truth. Instead of trying to hear God and draw closer to Him through their dreams, people used them like divination—a source of fortune-telling to seize power, predict the future, and get more wealth. So the church discouraged individuals from paying attention to dreams.

The prophet Daniel knew God spoke through dreams when he prayed for interpretation of King Nebuchadnezzar's dreams (see Dan 2:17-23, 28). Church Father Irenaeus[i] declared that dreams give us revelation of the spiritual world and demonstrate we can be very close to God. He gives us visions and dreams through which He conveys the likeness of His nature and His glory.[33]

Closer to God

Working with our dreams can bring us into a closer, more intimate relationship with the living God. For example, Gerald said he felt particularly close to God in the following dream: "Walking along a quiet garden pathway, I met Pope John Paul II. We had a brief man hug, but after a few seconds, I started to draw back. When he continued to embrace me firmly, I decided to return the embrace.

From that moment I felt like I was receiving a divine hug—the deepest, most heart-touching, satisfying hug I have ever experienced. When I described the dream to Judith, I said, through tears of great joy and gratitude, that I felt like I had been hugged by Jesus."

---

i Christian Apologist, Irenaeus (c. 175-185), a native of Smyrna & bishop of Lyons, in "*Against Heresies*" comments on dreams and visions.

We can imagine that Daniel, when asked to interpret the dreams of the king, stayed very close to God. As we handle our dreams, we also must *maintain a humble reliance upon the Lord.*

Cultivate our faith

As with all aspects of our Christian walk, working with our dreams requires us to exercise faith—the confidence and assurance that we can trust God. The Bible makes it clear God speaks to people through dreams. So we can *cultivate our faith*, trusting that, if we do our part, He will illumine the significance of the dream message in the right time.

I view dream work as a collaborative effort between God and us. Recognizing that *the interpretation belongs to God* (Gen 40:8), we place into His hands the dream content and our strategies or methods. Whether we use the gifts of the Holy Spirit or apply strategies and techniques from this book, the Lord knows the best way for us to approach each dream.

The journey to understand dreams begins with prayer. This establishes an environment of trusting the Lord to guide us, and helps us to position our heart before Him in humility. We thank God for the dream and ask the Holy Spirit to help us comprehend its meaning.

1. Prepare yourself for dream work

- Consider dream work as time spent in the presence of God, a spiritual practice.
- Maintain a sense of sacredness—play music or light a candle as you begin dream work.
- Create an atmosphere of trusting the Holy Spirit to lead you.

2. Pray for understanding of your dream

- Acknowledge God's presence.
- Thank God for your dream.
- Humbly ask God for the interpretation of your dream.

🖃 21ˢᵗ c. dreamer—Ralph Nault

My friend Ralph Nault* struggled for several weeks with a heavy spirit. His joy was gone, everything seemed hard to do, even his ministry work that he loved. One night he dreamed:

I am digging in the shell of a building that has no foundation and no floor, trying to build a foundation under its edges. I strike a metal box that turns out to be a tiny casket that is making strange sounds and wobbling as it rises above the surface. A voice behind me says, "Here, this is yours," and someone hands me a tiny skeleton that is kicking and scream-ing in a shrill voice. It kicks free and begins to dance, leap, and somersault, shouting joyfully, "I'm free! I'm free! Praise God, I'm free!"

I realize the skeleton came from the casket, but it did not want to return. I feel as if I am the skeleton and know what it wants, thinks and feels. Suddenly I am myself again. In this moment, I realize that I and the skeleton are one.

After awakening, Ralph prayed for an interpretation of his dream. He immediately knew that the skeleton represents his spiritual man; his digging represents his own effort to build his spiritual house. The casket symbolizes the letter of the law—though good, it bound his spiritual man, robbing him of joy and freedom. The dream shows him that his spiritual man had become strong enough to break free from the laws, rules, regu-lations, and the fleshly practice of religion. The person who hands him the skeleton is the Holy Spirit, bringing him into a new place of freedom in Christ Jesus.[34]

* Ralph Nault closed his electrical contracting business and began ministering full-time as a Catholic lay evangelist. (See Nault's blog at http://www.ralphnault.com/blog/)

Part Two

Nighttime Dramas

Many of our dreams are like mini-dramas: stories unfolding during sleep that are metaphors for the events of our waking lives. Dreams can vary widely, from single images to complex, seemingly endless sagas. Whether our nighttime dramas take the form of a simple still shot or an elaborate movie production, we are usually one of the actors.

Part Two presents the fundamental concepts and principles that provide a Christian basis for your dream work. You will discover the many blessings of dreams and their divine purposes. You'll also learn how to identify the various types of dreams, and begin to appreciate the significance of each type of drama played out while you sleep. I describe the principles of symbolism, and suggest two ways to approach your dreams.

Dream work principles

☆ Most dreams are about you, not others.
☆ Sharing dreams with another supportive person is good practice.
☆ Behind dreams is an intelligent intent, urging us toward wholeness and holiness.
☆ Some dreams are far more important than others.
☆ Most dreams need to taken symbolically, not literally.
☆ Dreams require something from us: we must seek to find their hidden treasure.

Dear Jacob,

You wily rascal! Did you actually think you could outrun your brother, Esau, out here in the Luz/Bethel wilderness after you cheated him out of his birthright? Get real. If the man catches you, he will chew you up and spit you out in the dust.

Speaking of catching, I'm glad I caught up with you out here where it's quiet and peaceful. Maybe you can hear what I have to say. I've got quite a burden to dump on you, my friend. The dream I have for you is going to change your life forever—you'll never be the same again. Grab a nearby stone for your pillow and listen to this dream:

Jacob took one of the stones of the place and put it under his head, and lay down in that place. And he had a dream, and behold a ladder was set on the earth with its top reaching to heaven; and behold, the angels of God were ascending and descending on it.

And behold, the Lord stood above it and said, "I am the Lord, the God of your father Abraham and the God of Isaac; the land on which you lie, I will give it to you and to your descendants … I am with you, and will keep you wherever you go, and will bring you back to this land; for I will not leave you until I have done what I have promised you (Gen 28:11-16)."

Respectfully yours,

Yahweh

8

Most Dreams Are About You!

This was your dream and the visions in your mind while on the bed ... that you may understand the thoughts of your mind [lit. heart]. – Daniel 2:28-30

Our dreams are highly personal, uniquely reflecting us, the individual dreamer. Keep this principle uppermost in your mind: *Most of your dreams are about you, not others.* Because the dream feels *so* real, we often think it must be about the other person. But usually it's not.

This was one of my most challenging difficulties in unlocking the mystery of dreams. For example, my fig leaf dream (#2 *God, Did You Speak To Me During The Night?*) was about me, not about my friend making slipcovers. A shadow figure, she symbolized some aspect of myself.

What blessings do dreams bring us?

To ground my dream work in Christian beliefs, I reviewed the beliefs of the Church Fathers about dreams. Origen[j] believed that God provides dreams for the benefit of the one who had them *and* for those who hear them.[35] Synesius of Cyrene held that dreams give us wise counsel, announce good news, inform us against the worst, and help us with intellectual tasks and problem solving.[36]

Bishop Cyprian[k] claimed that God often used noticeable visions to guide and direct the councils of the church. He also emphasized direct personal encounters with God via dreams and visions.[37] One of my favorites, St. Augustine, who was known for good psychological insight, taught that dreams help us understand both human psychology and people's relationship to God.[38]

---

j Origen (c.185–254), one of the greatest Christian thinkers of the third century, declared in *Contra Celsus*, that many pagans had been converted to Christianity by means of dreams, by this kind of direct break-through into their lives in waking visions and dreams of the night.

k Church Father, Bishop Cyprian (c. 259) was a founder of the Latin Church and pupil of Tertullian. When a new wave of Christian persecution began, he was beheaded. However he was prepared to go because in his dream a young man of unusual stature told him what was going to happen to him.

Once in a while, someone may receive a dream with a very clear message for the whole body of Christ. In the majority of dreams, however, God is dealing with us as individuals, to reveal truth about ourselves, to edify and build us up. Whether they deal with external events or internal issues, our dreams will invite us to new understanding and insight—but they will never condemn us.

As a rule, your dreams will be concerned with the events and circumstances of your own life—your ideas about yourself, other people, and the world around you. Your dreams will be about your:

- Current situations and happenings at home and work.
- Concerns for family members and relationships.
- Emotional, mental, physical, and spiritual well-being.
- Choice of career, calling, and vocation.
- Relationship with God.

From experience with my own dreams, I found that many of them dealt with the struggles and concerns in my heart, my emotional issues, my unresolved life conflicts, and my spiritual understanding.

What do John Newton and Mother Teresa have in common?

Many of you know that John Newton was the author of *Amazing Grace* in the 18th Century. But do you know that he stopped being a slave-trading ship captain and became an Anglican clergyman because of a dream in the night?[39]

And of course you know of the work of Mother Teresa in the 20th century.[/] But do you know that she found the direction and energy for her ministry in a dream in which she encountered St. Peter at the gates of Heaven?[40]

Dreams tell the truth

Here is another principle: *The dream is trying to show us something we are unaware of, not something we already know.* Dreams don't waste your time—they show you something you need to know about yourself and your relationship with others, with God, and with the world around you.

/ Born Anjezë Gonxhe (1910–1997) of Albanian origin, she became a Roman Catholic Religious Sister and missionary known around the world as Mother Teresa. She lived most of her life in India, caring for the poor and dying; she founded the Missionaries of Charity, a Roman Catholic religious congregation, which in 2012 consisted of over 4,500 sisters active in 133 countries. (http://en.wikipedia.org/wiki/Mother_Teresa)

If you think you already know what your dream seems to be saying, perhaps you need to look again.

Here's an interesting dream from my friend, Margaret. Her husband had just left her and was planning to divorce her. Unable to accept it, she kept holding to the hope he'd return—for the glory of God. So she and I went on a camping trip to help her cope with the ensuing loss. One night in a Michigan campground, she dreamed she was back in Scotland, her native country: She is riding a tram, juggling large bulky bundles. She expects her husband to join her, as they had planned.

At every stop, she looks for him to get on the tram. Finally, when it becomes apparent that he isn't coming, she makes a decision and says to herself, "If he doesn't come by the time I get to the Glasgow Cathedral, I will go home and divorce him." Another female acquaintance on the tram offers to give her a makeover. As the tram arrives at the cathedral, she notices its grimy, dirty appearance is gone. Sandblasted, and with new landscaping, it looks glorious—to the glory of God.

Margaret's dream showed her the truth about her situation, something she hadn't been able to accept. The bundles represented her children (including a son with Down Syndrome) whom she'd have to continue to care for alone. The cathedral symbolized herself. Until this dream, she'd been unable to even say the word "divorce." But after the dream, she went on the offensive, retained her own lawyer, and filed for divorce herself. Eventually she emerged with a brand new life, a makeover.

1. Assume your dream is about you

Begin with the assumption that your dream is probably about something you are (should be?) dealing with right now. Most likely it is about specific events in your recent experience and your inner response to them.

- Consider how your dream relates to your current concerns.
- What does it tell you about your life right now? At home? At work?
- How does it portray your present relationships?
- Is the emotion in your dream similar to how you feel in some waking situation?
- Does the dream theme match any circumstance you are in?
- What implications does it have for your everyday waking life?

2. Dreams reveal something you don't know

Your dreams are trying to reveal the truth to you, perhaps something your mind cannot, or will not, accept. Ask yourself these questions:

- What am blind to that my dream trying to make me aware of?
- What truth is it bringing to me?
- What understanding does it bring me about my current situation?
- Does it offer insight into resolving a problem or issue?
- Does it provide direction about moving my life forward?

3. View your dream in context of your entire life—both background & future

To understand some dreams, you will need to consider them within the context of your entire life, not just your current concerns. Sweeping back over your life, reflect on how the dream may relate to your long-standing hopes, unresolved life experiences, intrapsychic conflicts, and divine promises.

- Is the dream trying to help you look at something from your past? Something not finished?
- How does it relate to any childhood experience? Does it take place in your childhood home?
- What may it be telling you about your calling, vocation, career choice?
- Is it trying to prepare you for something in the future? Expand your vision?
- Ask, why this dream at this particular time of your life?

▣ *19ᵗʰ c. dreamer—Abraham Lincoln*

President Abraham Lincoln (1809-1865), about two weeks before his assassination, dreamed the following:

Around the coffin were stationed soldiers who were acting as guards; and there was a throng of people, some gazing mournfully upon the corpse, whose face was covered, others weeping pitifully.

"Who is dead in the White House?" I demanded of one of the soldiers. "The President," was his answer. "He was killed by an assassin!"

Then came a loud burst of grief from the crowd, which awoke me from my dream.[41]

Dear Sergeant,

Since you've been a faithful soldier, I'm giving you a chance to avoid a massive defeat at the hand of my boys from Israel. There's no question that I have my favorites, and Gideon's Jerusalem gang tops my list. So here's how it goes.

I've prepared what I believe is a simple dream for you. If you get it right, you'll save yourself and your fellow insurgents a lot of grief. Talk about it with your friends and colleagues immediately—don't wait until Thursday's dream group to discuss its meaning. It's pretty important to understand this dream right away.[44]

A cake made of barley bread came rolling through the camp of Midian; it reached the tent, struck against it and turned it upside down (Judg 7:13)

Sincerely,

Yahweh, God of the Victorious Israelis

9

Dream Sharing

Joseph said to them, 'Do not interpretations belong to God? Tell it to me, please.' – Genesis 40:8

People around us often can recognize the meaning of our dream symbols better than we can. It is a paradox of dream work that the dream, this product of our most private and intimate being, may best be fully realized by sharing it with others.[42]

Sharing our dreams with another supportive person is good practice. Telling someone the dream fixes it in our memory, making recall easier. Often we can gain a better understanding of our dreams when we share them. In the Gideon story told in Judges 7, the Midianite soldier received the interpretation of his dream when he told it to his buddy.

Insight from others

We can also benefit from the insights and ideas of others. Since the dream expresses what is buried deep inside us, it's largely inaccessible to our rational mind. Although we are blind to the "log" in our own eye, other people are able to see our issues more clearly—especially if they are honest, intuitive, and open to the Holy Spirit.

In the mid 1980s, I had this dream: An unseen person is speaking to me, saying, "Study psychology; it will pay you big dividends."

Our good friends, Ralph and Pauline Nault, happened to be with us that morning, so I shared the dream with them. Immediately Ralph said, "It means metaphysical psychology!" Neither of us knew exactly what this meant, so we consulted a dictionary and learned that it has to do with essential reality—the nature of being, the origin of things.

As a result of this dream, I spent many hours reading and studying on this theme. Over time I realized that I had hold of the shadow, not the substance or essential reality God offers us. And I experienced transformation deep within my soul. "Study psychology" is an example of a clear dream giving direction. No interpretation needed. When I shared it with a friend, however, I received more clarity of its meaning.

We are the decision-maker

By depending upon the Holy Spirit and asking skillful questions, other people can help draw out the meaning of our dream. But we must never accept ideas for understanding our dream that our heart does not witness to. Sometimes phrases such as "prophetic interpretation of dreams," or "anointed interpretation" can be compelling. But it's up to us to decide what our dream means, if the prophet or teacher is right. If we give this responsibility to others, we are giving away our God-given right.

Don't let anybody else decide for you what your dream means. As you look repeatedly for patterns of symbols in your dreams over time, you'll devise your own dictionary of correct meanings for your dream symbols. The final word on what your dream symbols mean belongs to you.

1. Share your dream

Tell your dream to someone who appreciates the value of dreams as a way to hear from God. Say, "I had an interesting dream, and I want to know what God is saying to me. I'd like your ideas about what my dream might mean."

- What do you see in my dream?
- What area of my life do you think my dream is about?
- What do you think God is trying to show me, make me aware of?
- If you were in my life situation and this were your dream, what might it be telling you?

2. Read your dream aloud in the present tense

Another idea is to read your dream aloud, in the present tense, to another person. Sometimes saying something out loud helps us understand it better, leading to more insight, either cognitively or emotionally.

- Read dream aloud, using the present tense: "I am … "
- Recap its most important parts, allowing your emotions to connect to them.[43]
- Note what it moves within your soul as you read.
- Note any cognitive or emotional insights you experience.

10

Biblical Purposes

For He gives to His beloved even in his sleep. – Psalm 127:2

Testimony through the ages gives evidence that dreams have a divine purpose—to make us more fully alive, call us to holiness, help us become complete, whole persons, and bring us into a close relationship with God.[45] Christian psychologist David G. Benner describes dreams as communications from God containing messages intended to enhance our well-being. He says an *"intelligent intent" is behind our dreams, urging us toward wholeness and holiness.*[46]

Our Creator always has our best interests at heart, with plans for our well-being, to give us a future and a hope (Jer 29:11). Underlying dreams is the divine purpose of enlarging us—increasing the depth and scope of our lives. Recognizing the divine purposes of dreams in the Bible will give you a schema with which to consider what God may be trying to say to you. See Appendix A, *Dreams & Visions in the Bible*, for examples of the divine treasure dreams and visions brought to dreamers in the Old and New Testament eras.

Twelve Divine Purposes of Dreams

In my search to discover why God gives us dreams, I identified twelve broad purposes of dreams in the Scriptures.[m]

1) Make God known to us

In Numbers 12:6-8, God says He uses dreams to make Himself known to prophets. Isaiah, Jeremiah, Micah, Ezekiel, Zechariah, Peter, and Paul experienced God, receiving His living Word through visual experiences— either dreams or visions. God also used a dream to make Himself known to Jacob in his renowned angels-on-a-ladder dream (Gen 28:11-16).

---

m For more explanation and illustrations, see Judith Doctor, *Dream Treasure: Learning the Language of Heaven* (Chapter 10).

43

Many stories of Jesus revealing Himself in dreams to Muslims provide evidence God that still uses dreams to make himself known to people.

2) Make God's words known to us

God makes a wonderful promise in the Old Testament that He will pour out His Spirit and make His words known to us (Prov 1:23). Then in the New Testament at Pentecost, St. Peter connects the coming of the Holy Spirit with dreams, visions, and prophecies, providing avenues for God to make His words known to us (Acts 2:16). In our experience, we have found this to be true. God can speak to us on a very personal level through an incredible supranatural source—the dream!

Listen to this remarkable assertion by Early Orthodox Church Father, John Chrysostom:[n] "Dreams are a frequent source of revelation from the spiritual realm, and God reveals Himself through dreams. If we are finely tuned to God, we don't need visions or other more dramatic divine revelations—we can depend upon dreams to hear from God."[47]

3) Provide divine counsel—problem-solving dreams

My friend Rev. Herman Riffel said, "The dream is an invaluable counselor ... It is with us every night, charges no fee, and makes no demand except that we listen to it and learn to detect God's voice in symbolic language ... there is no better way to get to heart of our problem."[48]

During sleep our minds may be turned off, but our spirits are still active, listening as the Lord God offers us guidance and direction in our sleep. Jacob received counsel in his relationship with Laban via a dream, telling him what to do with the flock (Gen 31:10-29). Joseph dreamed of an angel telling him to not be afraid to take Mary as his wife, even though she was with child (Matt 1:20).

4) Give godly instruction—guidance dreams

In Job 33:15, Elihu told Job that, when sound sleep falls on men, God seals their instruction. According to Psalm 16:7, God also instructs us in the night. While we sleep, we receive His nightly instruction through dreams.

Although many dreams offer some type of guidance, there seem to be differences among them. For instance, instruction dreams give us clear

---

[n] John Chrysostom (c. 347–407), known as John the Golden-mouth, helped to form the mold for all Eastern Christianity down to the present. The Greek Church viewed his writings as nearly on a par with the Scriptures.

direction concerning something we need to do or where to go, or they emphasize something that is important. Typically we awake from such a dream with an inner knowing that God has spoken to us.

As a remarkable example, Harriet Tubman (1820-1913) received divine instruction through her dreams in the night. An escaped slave, she led hundreds of slaves to freedom through the "Underground Railroad" (a system of meeting spots maintained by antislavery advocates). Tubman made 19 rescue trips to the south in order to lead her people on their dangerous journey to the north, with slave-hunting patrols vigorously pursuing her. She said that her dreams helped her find the safe pathways and that she never lost a single "passenger."[49]

Think about how Joseph was instructed to take Mary as his wife in a dream and also was given the name to call his son (Matt 1:20-21). Then consider how St. Paul's vision in the night pointed him in the right direction: A certain man of Macedonia was ... appealing to him, ... "Come over to Macedonia and help us" (Acts 16:9).

I have stories like this of my own. In 2001, we sensed that we needed to live in Germany a while. A pastor in Braunschweig suggested we come there and teach about the ministry of inner healing. But we also had close contacts in southern Germany, so we were unsure where to move. We asked the Lord for clarity. Then I dreamed: With her arms outstretched, an unknown woman is calling out to me, "Come, we are so hungry!" In the dream, I knew this woman was from Braunschweig.

When I awoke, I knew our direction. The dream also gave us the faith and courage to sell our home and many belongings, and leave our family. In late 2001, we moved to Braunschweig and there I met the woman I'd seen in my dream. Shortly thereafter, the Lord opened the door to radio ministry in the south of Germany too.

5) Open our ears, get our attention—nightmares, trauma dreams, repetitive themes

Resistant to change, we often need help to open our ears to hear what God wants to say to us. One way God gets our attention is through dreams, according to Job's advisor, Elihu. He asserts that God speaks to us in dreams (even multiple times on the same subject) trying to get us to notice. Failing this, He may turn up the heat, bringing us frightening dreams or nightmares that jolt us into awareness (Job 33:14-18).

A nightmare—being chased, attacked, drowning, falling, fighting in a war zone—causes us to wake up feeling terrified. Palms sweating, heart pounding, we thank God it was only a dream! Usually the experience is not completed in the dream, suggesting we have unresolved issues.

Recurring nightmares are a signal that something is unhealed in our hearts. Since most nightmares don't just conveniently go away, we can take them to Our Lord to receive His healing grace. See #25 *Nightmares and Recurrent Motifs* for ways to deal with nightmares.

6) Change attitudes—keep us from pride

Our attitudes are deeply embedded in our memories, beyond our conscious minds, branded into our souls by our life experiences. Attitudes determine our view of ourselves and the world around us—we live the existence permitted by what we believe. If our attitudes are loaded with lies and illusions, they need replacement by healing, life-giving words from God.

Sometimes we need a dream to change our attitudes—in Job's case (Job 33:17), to prevent him from developing pride. Our dreams offer us a wonderful resource for exposing our negative attitudes and beliefs about our self and our place in the world. Fearful of taking his family to Egypt to visit his son Joseph, Jacob's attitude was changed by a dream. Because God promised to bring him back out again, Jacob broke free from his fear (Gen 46:1-7).

God also used a dream to change my husband's behavior. Gerald describes how God identified his wrong attitude in a dream: "Former NBA player, Bill Lambier, known for his rough basketball tactics, was shooting baskets. I said, 'They call you the last of the Big Bruisers.' He didn't like it, but I assured him that's what they call him. I felt God was showing me that my unkind demeanor and speech damaged my relationship with my wife and alienated my children. I prayed for restoration."

7) Change conduct and behavior

Elihu told Job he was privileged to hear from God in his dreams, because it enabled him to change unacceptable conduct. Dreams, the ever-present nighttime counselor, call our attention to attitudes, behaviors, values, and emotional reactions that are no longer life-giving. The intensity of the dream images—the evoked emotion—helps us discern our inner motivations, enabling us to change our behavior. For example, Laban was warned in a dream to be careful how he spoke to Jacob (Gen 31:24).

8) Keep our soul from death—warning dreams

Dreams may serve to warn us so that our lives are not destroyed. One of Elihu's arguments to Job was that, by heeding the warnings in his dreams, he might keep his soul in the land of the living (Job 33:18). In order to save both Israel and Egypt, Pharaoh dreamed of seven fat cows from the Nile River being eaten by seven lean cows (Gen 41:1-49).

Sometimes people's dreams indicate potential injury to themselves. But this does not necessarily mean it will happen—there's no predictive power that makes evil things happen. Warning dreams may be given so the event doesn't occur. In the Christmas story, God warned the magi in a dream not to return to Herod, so they took an alternative route home (Matt 2:12).

Diagnostic dreams

Dreams about our physical body are often challenging. Fortunately, dreaming of dying is usually a metaphor for psychological change—something within us needs to die. God may use dreams, however, to provide insight into bodily conditions, alerting us to impending physical problems even before symptoms are evident.

My friend, Pauline Nault, had decided not to have her female organs removed—even though the doctor insisted she needed it. She wanted to wait for God to heal her, until she dreamed: Her house was sliding off its foundation, while she frantically was trying to save her treasures. She knew something was wrong with its water system. Recognizing that this dream symbolically portrayed her problem, she scheduled the surgery!

Nearly two millennia earlier, renowned 2nd century Greek physician, Galen, recognized the diagnostic value of dreams. He even switched his major from philosophy to medicine as a result of dreams. He operated numerous times based on dreams, and claimed it saved many lives.[50]

9) Enlighten with the light of life—energizing, comforting, encouraging dreams

Job 33:30 indicates that God may shine His living light on us in the dream. When that happens, we're more fully alive, able to do more than we ever imagined. By transforming the powerful energy contained within us into images and symbols, our dreams can energize us for everyday living—help us complete unfinished projects, release creativity, provide enthusiasm for new activities.

Life can be tough. We need encouragement along the way. God may grace us with gifts of encouragement or comfort in a dream. We may also be graced with spiritual gifts, such as faith, wisdom, or anointing for ministry.

In my experience, dreams carry divine energy that can create hope and faith in our hearts to empower us for living. Although most death dreams are subjective (about our internal world), occasionally people may dream of a recently deceased loved one. Called "gift dreams," they bring comfort and peace into the heart of a bereaved person.[51]

Dr. Len Sperry[o] tells about a mother's dream that took place in heaven a few days after her son's death: "Her completely healed son bounded across an open, sunny field to greet her. He wanted to tell her he 'was doing fine, that God was OK,' and that he was with two elderly, loved neighbors."[52]

10) Reveal divine mysteries—spiritual revelation dreams

Daniel assured King Nebuchadnezzar that God reveals mysteries in dreams (Dan 2:28-30). We cannot understand divine mysteries with our natural minds; they can be known only through revelation. In my experience, spiritual revelation dreams give us a deeper understanding of the life, death, and resurrection of Christ—the gospel is made more fully explicit to us, enabling us to grasp its full significance for our lives.

These dreams arise from beyond the structure of our soul, from the Spirit of God. We can recognize this type of dream since the symbolism is charged with great energy and often has religious connotations like an angel, a crucifix, Bible, church, monastery, altar, priest, bread and wine, or Jesus Himself. Because they bring revelation about spiritual matters, these dreams produce transformation deep within us—however, they are quite rare.

Here is a dream that I was blessed with: I am being chased by some type of shadowy figure near the house my father build. Terrified, I run toward my dad's house. The figure continues to follow me. I run into the house and slam the door shut. When I turn around, the shadowy thing is there. I turn toward it and ask who it is. As I reach out and touch it, I suddenly know who it is. I say, "You are the ark of the covenant ... and I know who the ark of the covenant is: it's Jesus!"

---

o Len Sperry, M.D., PhD, has written 60 professional books on various health topics, including the practice of spiritually-oriented psychotherapy.

Very simply, I am the house my Father God has built—I contain the living Christ in me.

11) Foretell the future—prophetic dreams

Another biblical purpose of dreams is to announce or warn about future situations before they actually happen (see Dan 2:28-29). Also called anticipatory dreams, they may give answers or offer solutions, or they may suggest a pessimistic turn of events.

Benefit an individual

Some prophetic dreams tell individuals about specific future events, providing information outside of their own experience. Perhaps, instead of predicting the future, their purpose is to help someone become aware of what God is doing when something happens. A young field hand named Joseph received two dreams from God about his future destiny (Gen 37:7,9).

Dreams about future happenings also can prepare us for necessary action and call us to intercession. Or they might be simply telling us what will happen *if we don't change* in some way. Understanding this type of dream relies upon our spiritual senses. Another way is whether or not the dream comes true.

One more caution: Don't be afraid to test the interpretation of someone else's dream about you (see #32 *Test Your Interpretation*).

Benefit community, church, or nation

While most dreams deal with everyday lives, some may have far-reaching significance to more people than just the dreamer. Known as "big" dreams or prophetic dreams, they foretell in accurate detail specific future events of importance for whole groups of people.

Prophetic dreams may appear when some dimension of God's plan is at stake, so people will know what to do when unexpected difficulties arise. Pharaoh's dream made him aware of approaching famine and gave him time to prepare for it, so whole groups of people could be preserved alive (Gen 41:1-4).

Prophetic dreams are extremely rare. The best advice I can give you is this: If you think your dream is for the larger community, pause and take a deep breath—it's probably about you. Ask the Lord how your dream might relate to your personal struggles. I also encourage you to seek advice from wise people who are sensitive to God's Spirit. And never use prophetic dreams to control others or to bring them under your authority.

12) Reveal innermost thoughts and intentions of the heart

One unique purpose of King Nebuchadnezzar's dream was to show him what was in his heart—what was going on in his inner life—so that perhaps he would repent and change (see Dan 2:28–30). This type of dream acts like a mirror, reflecting current attitudes, thoughts, and intentions of the heart.

This is *the divine purpose of many of our dreams: to reveal what's going on in our own heart.* This type of dream helps us discover the truth about our self, our motivations, and become psychologically honest. Way ahead of modern psychology, Basil the Great[p] understood that the inner workings of the personality are often revealed in dreams.[53]

By revealing what is happening in your heart, the dream enables you to make a connection between your inner psycho-spiritual life and the choices you are making in your outer life. Dreams can help you to connect with God's plan for your life and see your choices more clearly.

Connect With Divine Purpose of Dream

From our discussion of the broad scope of biblical purposes of dreams, it's evident that dreams offer help for every dimension of our lives. Because God loves us, He has given us a marvelous capacity—the ability to hear Him speak directly to us in the nighttime. God offers us this grand gift through which He conveys His wisdom, guidance, and counsel.

Understanding the biblical purpose of our dreams helps put us in touch with God's purpose for our lives, revealing how He is leading us toward godliness and wholeness. I hope you're becoming as excited about the dream as I am!

1. Ask questions to help you reflect on the biblical purpose of your dream

- "God, what are you trying to say to me through this dream?"
- Why did this particular dream come to me just now?

---

p Basil the Great (329-379), an archbishop of Caesarea, was a great Christian theologian and Church Doctor in the East.

- What primary life issue might my dream drama be related to?
- Which of the divine purposes might my dream best fit into?
- Have you dreamed this same theme or motif before?
- "God, is there any invitation for me in this dream?"

⊟ 5ᵗʰ c. dreamer— Roman physician Gennadius

St. Augustine tells two dreams experienced by Gennadius, a former Roman physician, in a letter written in 414 A.D. At the time, Gennadius was troubled about the existence of life after death.

In the first dream, a young man beckoned Gennadius to follow him. Hearing music of unsurpassed beauty, Gennadius inquired of his guide and was told, "It is the hymn of the blessed and the holy."

On the following night the same youth appeared in Gennadius' dream and asked Gennadius if he knew him and where they had met. Gennadius correctly identified the previous night's dream as the place they had met; he recalled the exquisite music and knew he'd been dreaming the events. Upon further questioning, Gennadius was aware that he was presently sleeping and in his bed.

The youth explained to Gennadius that, although his eyes of his body were not seeing because he slept, he had other eyes to see the events of his dreams. Similarly, after death, his body's eyes would not see, but he would have faculties to perceive. The youth warned Gennadius to stop doubting the continuance of life after death.[54]

11

How Important Is This Dream?

Dreams are "a combination of messages about the state of the inner world and fragments of life experiences that are shaped by God as a communication designed for our well-being." – David Benner[55]

O ften I get asked, "Are all dreams equally important?" No, they're not. *Some dreams have far-reaching consequences for your life*; others don't. God deals with our lives in a many ways, some seemingly small, some evidently more consequential. How do you tell the difference?

Eight Types of Dreams

Recognizing the different types or categories of dreams will also help you determine the significance of a dream. In this section you'll learn to identify eight dream categories often delineated by dreamworkers. *Notice that, in each dream type, I give you a suggested approach for how to work with it.*

1) Routine maintenance dreams

Keeping our house from deteriorating takes a lot of daily cleaning and maintenance. Dreams are like that. Much of our nighttime imagery involves keeping our internal house functioning properly. Our dreams are trying to equalize, balance, or adjust our consciousness in a purposeful manner, helping restore inner equilibrium and release psychic energy. We need dreams just to stay stable and steady, and to release unexpressed emotions and thoughts.

Dream research emphasizes the vital importance of dreaming to mental health and well-being. Deprived of dreaming in our sleep, tension builds inside, and we tend to become unstable and irritable. So be thankful for all those dreams you can't remember or make sense of—they keep you sane.

We are not often aware of routine maintenance dreams—they just don't seem to grab our attention when we awaken. *But if you become aware of one, take time to prayerfully reflect on it.* I have found that even my seemingly insignificant dreams have something to offer me.

2) Current event dreams

Current event dreams comment on what's happening in our daily lives and help us work through problems and issues. These dreams can be dramatic representations of inner conflicts or aspirations. Such dreams help us become more conscious and aware, showing us something we need to see. Episcopalian priest, Rev. John A. Sanford,[q] suggests they enable us to "sort out the events that transpired the day before, or prepare us for the day to come."[56]

To understand current event dreams you must have an accurate understanding of your existing state of affairs. You need to be familiar with your recent experiences, prayers, dilemmas, and aspirations, and to reflect honestly on your current concerns and emotional reactions.

3) Historic event dreams

Some of our dreams are dealing with unresolved, forgotten or repressed experiences in our lives. This type of dream helps us find the light of God's love and truth about long-ago events, so we can make peace with unsettled conflicts or find healing from traumatic experiences.

Understanding historic event dreams calls for you to reflect honestly on your history: recall childhood events, relationships with parents, attitudes and beliefs learned in childhood or in a previous relationship.

Exploring historic dreams is similar to looking through old photos. We allow personal memories and feelings to float to consciousness until we find the conflict or trauma that matches the emotional energy in our dream.

During a time of inner healing, I dreamed the following: I am in the backyard of my childhood home when I see a large tree (with no branches, only the trunk) walking toward me. It has eyes and is looking right at me. Terrified, I run into the house, trying to escape it. But the tree follows me inside. I run out the front door and down the sidewalk. As I run, I become an inch worm.

---

q Rev. John A. Sanford (1929- 2005), Episcopal priest, son of Agnes Sanford (founder of the Inner Healing Movement), authored books on serious dream study and interpretation.

I actually lived in this house until I was about 12 years old. Typically a childhood home depicts the part of our character which developed in our home environment, or things we experienced in that home as we grew up. I knew the tree symbolized my family tree. The dream was showing me that, if I wanted to become fully alive and free, I needed to explore my family history and the experiences I made during that time.

4) Archetypal (transformational) dreams

Archetypal[r] dreams are profound dreams with extraordinary potential and power. Coming from a deeper place within us, they indicate the possibility of a new development or transformation within ourselves. This type of dream emerges to assist us at different points along our journey. Larger than life, archetypal dreams present themes almost too powerful to hold in our mental grasp.

Understanding archetypal dreams may require knowledge of archetypal and transformational symbols. These images may come from outside the realm of ordinary experience—things you've never known in waking life. In some cases, however, common dream symbols can serve an archetypal purpose, such as discovering a previously unknown room in an unknown house, or driving a strange vehicle.

Here is an archetypal dream that Gerald received during a time of intense spiritual searching: "In a cathedral bell tower a sleeping giant was slumped over the bell. He slid out of the north side of the tower onto a flatbed trailer. The giant was paraded around the block, and then he entered the south side of the bell tower. As he entered, I discovered his cloak lying in the bottom of the bell tower. I was going to simply hand the giant his cloak, but a priest off to my left suggested I demand access to the giant in exchange for return of his cloak.

I believe the giant represents my God-given potential, asleep, unaware, in the bell tower pointing toward God. I've discovered his cloak, his mantle of authority. The part of me that relates to God stands close by, offering the possibility of using the cloak to gain access to the inner giant."

Archetypal symbols you may encounter in dreams:

* Characters such as giants, wise figures, precocious children, king/queen, angels, monks, priests, pregnant women, newborn baby, prisoner, lovers.

---

r St. Augustine labeled as "archetypes" the psychological patterns of energy within each one of us.

- Animals could be unicorns, mythical creatures, brilliantly plumaged birds, talking animals, snakes.
- Objects include chalice, rainbow, caves, churches, lightning, church bells, graveyard, clouds, sword.
- Themes might be marriage ceremony, giving birth, redemption, temptation,
- Activities could include ocean journey, mountain climbing, treasure hunting, city under siege.

Benefitting from archetypal dreams

To benefit from the transformational energy embedded in our archetypal dream, we must both:

1. Experience the emotion carried by the image (only emotion has the energy to cause the necessary changes in us).
2. Understand the symbolic significance of the image (the way the emotional content helps bring our choices to consciousness).

5) Divine encounter dreams

Divine encounter dreams are the most important, because they directly connect us with the living God. We never forget this type of dream experience.

Unlike ordinary dreams, divine encounter dreams transcend our personal lives and come from deep in our own spirit or from the Spirit of God. They affect us deeply, because they bring insight and revelation about spiritual matters. Sometimes called spectacular dreams or numinous dreams (expresses the idea of holiness or awesomeness), they "go beyond dealing with every day events and concerns to access our spirituality."[57]

In this type of dream, we directly encounter something from the spiritual world—God, angelic beings, or Jesus in human form. When we awaken, we intuitively know the dream was unusual because it affects us so deeply. Often this type of dream is associated with major life changes, and sometimes with religious conversion.

Many people of faith in the Western world have lost touch with religious symbolic experience. De-symbolized, they do not know how to allow the symbolic material in their dreams to come alive with meaning. *Understanding divine encounter dreams requires a deep spiritual sense and knowledge of our inner world.*

This divine encounter dream gave me revelation of what it means to flow with the Holy Spirit: The angel Gabriel was teaching me to fly. I had wings strapped on my arms, and I was being taught to fly using the currents and the winds. I was very afraid, but I was flying. But when I took my eyes off the angel's instruction, I fell.

6) Extrasensory perception dreams

Extrasensory perception (ESP) dreams enable us to access information outside our experience, across time and space. They may tell us about future events, possibly our life's purpose. Perhaps their purpose is to make us aware of what God is doing when something happens.

This kind of dream may come to prepare us for necessary action and call us to intercession. Or it could be simply telling us what will happen, if we don't change in some way. Anticipatory dreams prepare, announce, or warn about certain future situations, often long before they actually happen."[58] Some anticipatory dreams may give answers or offer solutions, while others may suggest a pessimistic, even disastrous, turn of events.

Extrasensory perception dreams about specific events, especially predictive dreams, have a different quality to them. You just seem to know they mean something out of the ordinary. *A simple test of dreams purporting to foretell the future is whether or not they come true.*

In 1992, I dreamed of a phone call from my oldest brother, telling me that my mother was dying and her skin was yellow. Six months later I received a phone call from my brother exactly like the dream. My mother had six weeks to live! Her skin was yellow. I took comfort, because the Lord had prepared me for this shock.

Occasionally someone will have a dream that allegedly delivers a message for other people (individual or group). It's very important to remember that the dream still belongs to the dreamer, and has many levels of meaning for them, in addition to any message it may have for others.[59]

7) Clear dreams

In contrast to symbolic dreams, clear dreams are completely understandable, because they have no symbolic imagery that needs to be interpreted—they simply are what they are. Clear dreams seem to bring us a direct message from God, connecting us with His divine purpose. Not so common, clear dreams often consist of just a single image or scene. *Understanding this type of dream requires spiritual recognition and the witness of the Holy Spirit.*

8) Lucid dreams

This type of dream is not very well known in our culture, but I've had a few people ask about it. In lucid dreams, we realize right in the dream that we are actually dreaming. This type of dream offers us the possibility of taking a certain action or making a decision right in the dream.

Recognizing Important Dreams

Obviously divine encounter dreams will impact you more than routine maintenance dreams. Another clue to the importance of a dream is the intensity of its imagery (see #20 *Dream Intensity*). The more intense the symbols, the more important and urgent the dream message is. We also need to pay attention to our nightmares and repeated dream motifs. A recurring theme indicates that something happening in us is appealing for special consideration or expression (see #25 *Nightmares and Recurrent Motifs*).

Keep in mind that the length of a dream doesn't always signify its importance. Short or seemingly small dreams can carry great import for our lives—even if they don't seem to be very intense. The bottom line: ask God to show you which dreams should receive more attention.

1. Consider the importance of your dream

These questions will help you evaluate the importance of your dream:

- Can you identify which category your dream best fits in?
- Did you encounter something from the spiritual realm?
- How intense was the dream and its imagery?
- Have you dreamed this same theme or motif before?
- Did you awaken in terror?
- How important is it for you to consider this dream?

▤ 20ᵗʰ c. dreamer—Eric Metaxas

Not long ago, I came across an amazing dream shared by author and cultural commentator, Eric Metaxas (1963-). Practice exercise: What type of dream do you think this is?

"I was ice-fishing … I looked into the large hole we'd cut into the ice and saw the snout of a fish poking out. I reached down and picked it up by the gills and held it up. It was a large pickerel or perhaps even a pike.

In the dazzlingly bright sunlight shining through the blue sky and off the white snow and ice onto the bronze-colored fish, it appeared positively golden. But then I realized that it didn't merely look golden; it actually was golden. It was a living golden fish, as though I were in a fairy tale.

Right in the dream, I suddenly understood that this golden fish was Ichthys—Jesus Christ Son of God Our Savior. Right then, I realized He was real … at long last my search was over. I was flooded with joy."[60]

12

The Language of Dreams

Hear now My words: If there is a prophet among you, I the Lord ... shall speak with him in a dream. Not so, with My servant Moses ... with him I speak mouth to mouth ... and not in dark sayings. – Numbers 12:6-8

Here is where we have the most difficulty. We make the mistake of thinking that dreams communicate the same way as our rational brains. Most dreams don't.

Seldom is a dream message conveyed in clear, straight-forward speech. Instead dreams consist of symbolic imagery that moves and flows and unfolds. Usually the message is obscure, composed in metaphorical and allegorical language. This challenges our Western intellects, because we mistakenly want to take dreams at face value. A fundamental premise of dream interpretation says that *most dreams need to taken symbolically, not literally.* This should not surprise us.

The Bible provides compelling evidence that it is God who makes dreams obscure. In Numbers 12:6-8 (NASB), God says He will speak in dreams using a language of "dark sayings." Modern Bible translations typically say "puzzle" because It refers to mysterious speech presenting an enigma, a knotted message to be unraveled, like a proverb or a riddle.[61]

Understand symbolic language

A symbolic dream uses picturesque images, consisting of figures of speech, metaphors, similes, hyperboles and puns, to express its message. People, characters, animals, objects, vehicles, buildings in our dreams are symbolically portraying either our outer life or inner world.

The essence of symbolic language is that something tangible is used to make present something not easily perceived. To help us understand invisible spiritual realities, Jesus used ordinary tangible things—fire, trees, fish, candles, seeds, houses, rocks, wind—in His parables. Theologian Paul Tillich recognized that man's ultimate concern must be expressed symbolically, because only symbolic language can express the ultimate.[62]

For example, Apostolic Father, Polycarp of Smyrna,[s] while praying, received a symbolic vision of what was to happen to him. Seeing the pillow under his head burning, he realized that this signified his own impending death.[63]

Symbols evoke emotional response

The basis of symbolism is analogy: something difficult to communicate is understood by association with something concrete. Our lives are filled with symbols, like wedding rings, baby shoes, family heirlooms, photo albums—objects that are significant because they evoke emotional response deep within us. By embodying invisible truths and experiences in symbolic form, these visible objects point to, and make present to us, another unseen, invisible reality.

Symbols are not as easily manipulated by our rational mind as are words or concepts—symbols function at a deeper, more primary level. They belong to the language of our inner world and the spiritual dimension.

Anything in life that cannot be grasped by the intellect strives for realization through symbolism (Unknown).

Savary, Berne, & Williams describe a dream symbol as any image that evokes our emotional response, either during or after a dream. What grabs our attention is the energy that's inherent in a symbol.[64] Charged with emotional energy, a symbol becomes a message capable of delivering a profound religious idea or concept through our inner senses.

A dream symbol may be any visual image, a sound or a smell that elicits an emotional response in us—either during the dream or following it. Activities and experiences such as flying or falling can also be treated as symbols.

In the Scriptures, prophetic dreams were usually symbolic, both in their content and in how their stories develop. Unlike the transparency shown by clear or literal dreams, in prophetic dreams we don't know immediately whatever the symbolic image refers to.

Symbols do not have a fixed meaning

No matter how a particular symbol was used in the Bible, we do not rely upon a fixed meaning for any symbol. Every symbol has many possible

---

s Polycarp of Smyrna (c. 69–c.155 A.D.) was a Christian bishop who was martyred.

meanings and associations. Our challenge is to find out what that image means to us in our individual inner world.

A fish could represent: feeding of five thousand, Jesus Christ or Christianity, something coming from the depths of the unconscious, or the healing Christ living in the ocean of the heart. For me, growing up in a commercial fishing family, the fish might symbolize my family's livelihood, my father who smelled of fish every evening, or my love of water.

1. Apply the cardinal principles of symbolism

To unlock the meaning of a symbol, we must learn how to apply the cardinal principles of symbolism: intensity and personal association.

- Intensity refers to the emotional energy evoked by a symbol, the *felt feeling response*. It is the intrinsic power embedded in the symbol that enables transformation of our innermost being. (See #20 *Dream Intensity* for more on dream intensity.)
- Personal association enables us to determine what the objects, animals, and people in a dream mean to us in our inner world. (See #29 *Make Personal Associations* for how to make personal associations.)

2. Identify any figures of speech

Become familiar with the figures of speech so you can recognize them when they appear in a dream.

- Consider if a word or object could have another completely different meaning.
- Can you identify any puns in your dream?

3. Consider the dream as a metaphor

Many dream stories or dramas can be understood as a metaphor in motion.

- What kind of life situation might this dream depict?
- In what way does this dream reflect your current situation?
- Why would the dream have used just these images?

▤ 19th c. dreamer— Friedrich von Kekulé

Friedrich A. Kekulé (1829-1896), whose discoveries revolutionized organic chemistry, is perhaps best known popularly for his dream of snakes holding their tails that led to understanding the structure of the benzene ring. His most important single contribution, however, was his structural theory of organic composition (1857-8), which also came in part from a dream.

He describes "atoms gamboling before my eyes," observing how smaller atoms united to form pairs, larger atoms embraced the smaller ones, making chains of atoms, all involved in a "giddy dance." Awakening from his dream, Kekulé sketched on paper these dream forms he had seen.

In a speech given at the Deutsche Chemische Gesellschaft (German Chemical Society) in 1890, he described his dream. Excited by his discovery, Kekulé said to his colleagues, *"Let us learn to dream!"*[65]

13

Two Approaches

Yes, the interpretation of our dream belongs to God. But keep in mind that God deliberately keeps His wisdom hidden from us, and something is required of us in order to find it. We must seek it out.

For most dreams, the meaning is not on the surface. It's just not handed to us on a silver platter. King Solomon understood this when he said that God seems to enjoy hiding things. But he also said that it's rewarding for us to diligently search and discover those hidden treasures.

Simplify dream work

By now you must be a little overwhelmed with all the information I've loaded you with. So let's try a straightforward method to simplify dream work. Here are two ways to look at your dream:

1. What is it saying to me about my outer, everyday life?
2. What is it trying to show me about my inner world, my soul or personality?

We're starting with the premise that a dream is portraying some aspect of either your outer world (objective) or your inner world (subjective). Since the relationship to your outer life is more readily understood, I recommend that you work first with the objective aspect of your dreams.

1) Take an objective approach

When we take an objective approach, we look to see what the dream is reflecting about our everyday life—the external situations and experiences going on in our outer world. Our dream images refer to objects and events in our external world: people, circumstances, situations, and relationships in our waking life. The people may represent themselves, and the dream tells us something about them that is true, or something about our relationship with them that we are not seeing correctly.

If you dream about a neighbor or a boss, it might be calling attention to something in your association with them, perhaps an attitude you hold toward them. If you are currently in conflict with the person who appears in the dream, you might benefit from taking the dream quite literally.

Sometimes people and situations in the dream may involve actual events beyond your individual life, perhaps an entire community. But the most common type of objective dream deals with your own life issues. The dream comments on your exterior life and your relationship to it.

Three objective dreams

I am amazed when I come across dreams that resulted in something awesome in the outer world. Here are three incredible dreams:

1. In the 11th century, Bishop Bruno, who later became Pope Leo IX, dreamed of a hideously deformed old woman taunting him. He made the sign of the cross over her and she was transformed into a lovely woman. He understood that the woman represented the deplorable condition of the church. During his pontificate, the church was restored to its original beauty.

2. In the 16th century, Sir Thomas White, a London alderman, dreamed about founding a college where he saw three elm trees growing out of a single root. During his travels, he discovered an elm tree in Oxford. Deciding it was the elm in his dream, he bought a building and opened a hall for scholars. Later, in a former convent in Oxford, he discovered an elm with three trunks growing from the same root. Purchasing the land, he founded St. John's College.[66]

3. In the late 20th century, this dream was recounted in *Woman's Day*. After several miscarriages, a woman became pregnant, but was paranoid she would lose this baby too. She asked the Lord to reassure her that He would be with her regardless of what happened. That night she dreamed: She saw herself giving birth to a baby girl, and she heard the words, "All will be well." Peace flooded her when she awoke. Later, she gave birth to a baby girl on Christmas day.[67]

Considerations indicating an objective approach:

*   All details of the dream are virtually the same as in waking life.
*   Person in the dream is an immediate family member.
*   You are emotionally related to the person in the dream.
*   Person is depicted as in actual waking life, at their current age.

+ You are an observer, not participating in the action.
+ Dream simply doesn't fit subjectively.

2) Use a subjective approach

In using a subjective approach, we consider what this dream is trying to show us about our inner world. The dream uses places, characters, and objects from our outer world to depict symbolically what is going on deep within us. People, animals, circumstances, and situations are portraying some part of our inner structures, the dynamic processes within our own soul or heart.

A subjective dream

In the late 1970s, I was aware I had many emotional and psychological symptoms that indicated something was wrong inside. I asked the Lord to show me my true condition. He answered me in a dream: I am lying flat on a table, split open right down the middle. My insides are filled with rottenness, and hands are packing me with salt.

As I awoke, I immediately knew the meaning of my dream. I was rotten on the inside. My soul needed restoring. I remember praying, "God, I am sick from head to toe, and I do not know how to heal myself. I surrender myself to You. You are the great physician. Would you heal me?"

In another dream, I saw a wretched looking woman. I knew she symbolized the condition of my soul.

Considerations suggesting a subjective approach:

+ Dream is depicted differently from waking life.
+ Person is not emotionally important to you (but not *always* the case—it *may* be someone close to you).
+ Person belongs to your past or is a distant relative.
+ Person is someone famous.
+ Person is a stranger to you.
+ Dream simply doesn't fit objectively.

1. What does my dream reflect about my everyday outer life?

To explore how a dream reflects your waking life, ask questions like:

• Does the description fit anyone in my life or a circumstance currently in my life?
• Am I currently in conflict with this person?

- What metaphorical comment might my dream be making on my everyday events?
- What implications does it have for my waking life?
- What truth is it trying to bring me about the situations I am currently in?
- Am I being invited to reflect on more life-giving ways to live my life?

2. What does my dream show me about my inner world?

To reflect on what the dream might say about your inner life, ask questions like:

- What goes on inside me that this dream speaks of?
- What inner states of mind, attitudes, habits might the person suggest?
- In what situations do I behave like them?
- How am I like this person?
- Do I have the same gifts, talents, or possibilities as they do?
- What part of me has that capability, potential, quality?

◨ 21st c. dreamer— Rev. J. Lee Grady

J. Lee Grady, ordained minister, author, and former editor of *Charisma* magazine, dreamed that he was inside the Vatican when a tsunami turned the building upside down.

As he walked out on the ceiling, he met a group of priests and nuns with hands raised, singing choruses and fervently worshipping God. He felt the dream meant the Lord wants to send another wave of the Spirit that will turn the church upside down.[68]

Note: If we took Grady's dream subjectively, we might think that the Vatican represents his own life, his soul, or his inner world.

Part Three

Dream Processing

Dream processing refers to using a series of questions to draw out the visible information in the dream drama. Then we try to see how this information relates to what's currently happening in our lives—what parallels can we make to our outer life or inner world?

Christian dream work is not just about remembering our nighttime dramas; it's about what we *do* with the information in them. Processing our dreams helps us see how we are relating to the world around us and where we need to make some changes. It enables us to make connections between our heart and the choices we make in life.

We can use our dream work as a way to listen to God. Dream processing can show us areas of our life where God is trying to help us, enabling us to bring these areas to Him for His transforming grace and truth.

Dream work principles
☆ Many dreams follow a story pattern of four parts.
☆ Drawing offers a nonverbal approach to dream processing.
☆ The emotional feeling in a dream provides an important clue to unlocking the mystery of a dream.
☆ Processing dream actions helps us reflect on how we are relating to life.
☆ By observing our dream ego figure, we get an amazing perspective on how we behave in various situations in our daily life.
☆ The words or thoughts in a dream offer simple clues in our discovery process.
☆ The more intense the symbols, the more important the dream message is.

Dear Franklin,

I know living in a gated community, courtesy of the Pharaoh, has been a little uncomfortable for you. I've got some good news for you. Your prison days are about to become history. But next time you share your dream in group, try to kinda keep your enthusiasm tamped down a little. Go gently with your colleagues, especially Bob, the baker. That's all I can say about that for now.

Before you got thrown into the slammer, you were brewing up some pretty good stuff. Pharaoh seemed particularly to like the Nile Pale Ale and the late-harvest Merlot. Just a hint for you about where to restart your work. The dream I have for you goes like this:

The wine taster dreamed he saw a grape vine with three branches that shot forth blossoms and buds and clusters of fruit. Pressing the grapes, he presented the cup of wine to Pharaoh (Gen 40:10-11).

Sincerely yours,

Yahweh

14

Dream Stories

*Therefore, I speak to them in parables, because, while seeing they do not see,
and while hearing they do not hear, nor do they understand ... for the heart
of this people has become dull. – Matthew 13:13,15*

Similar to the structure of parables[t] told by Jesus, *many dreams follow
a familiar story pattern of four parts:* setting, plot development, culmination of plot, and conclusion. This simple four-part breakdown gives
you a straightforward, systematic approach to understand the structure
of your pillow story.

To process the dream, focus on each of the four parts individually. Use
a series of questions to draw out the information already visible in the
dream, and then link it to your outer life or inner world. Understanding
these four parts gives you a basis for further exploration.

Here is an example of a four-part dream story. Buried in a mid-life
crisis, Gerald said he felt as if his life was careening out of control. Everything was in a state of confusion and frustration inside. He was miser-
able—and so was everyone else near him. He wondered how he would
survive this mess he was in.

One night he had this dream: "Driving my little red sedan at high
speed, I run over a cliff and plunge down a perilously steep slope. My car
clips the edge of a group of trees and plunges crazily through thickets.
However, I am able to use brakes and steering to control my descent,
until my vehicle finally comes to rest near the bottom."

Accurately reflecting the out-of-control condition of his life at that
time, his dream indicated the danger he was in. However, it also offered
him hope and encouragement. Despite some close calls, he would make
it through this difficult time of life alive.

---

t A parable is a short story designed to teach some truth, conveying meaning indirectly by use of
   comparison or analogy.

Part One: Opening scene (dream setting)

As the curtain lifts on a dream, typically it first creates the context, sets the stage where a particular concern will unfold. People who will participate in the drama are introduced, and the location is established. Then the dream sets up the initial situation for the dreamer.

Not only does the dream setting form the backdrop for the dream action, but also it's an integral part of the content of the dream and its message. When the dream story opens, what's on stage depicts in metaphorical images an existing emotional status quo—and a hint of what may be disturbing it. Particular moods, certain time periods, or inner states of mind may be symbolized by the setting.

1. These questions will help you process the dream setting:
- Where is the dream taking place? Indoors or outdoors?
- Describe chief characteristics of setting: landscape, environment, colors, weather, time, season.
- Are there any natural elements such as water, sky, earth, fire?
- What usually takes place in this setting: leisure, work, daily life, worship?
- Does it remind you of any place you've been in waking life?
- What does this place bring to mind: memories, people, places, situations, experiences, words, ideas?
- How does the dream setting relate to your outer world now?

Part Two: Plot development (dream theme)

The plot (the middle segment or developmental sequence) sets up the theme of the dream, the problem or issue to be faced. As the plot unfolds, you (or the other dream characters) engage in the struggle to resolve the conflict. It shows how the issue impacts your life and how you mobilize your resources to cope with it.

2. Process plot development using questions like these:
- What is going on in the dream, the theme: dilemma, problem, issue, conflict?
- Describe the basic theme in a brief sentence.
- Have you ever been in this situation before?
- What does this theme bring to mind: people, experiences, places, words, ideas?

- How does the theme relate to your current problems, issues, struggles?
- What might the dream be trying to make you aware of?
- What kind of life situation are you in that might lead to creating this metaphorical drama?
- Is there a parallel between the theme and the ways you cope throughout your life?

Part Three: Culmination of plot (a because factor?)

As the story evolves, there is a pivotal point where the plot turns—something decisive happens (or doesn't) *because* of some crucial reason. Processing the "because factor" may help identify the source of an issue, perhaps even indicate a solution.

3. Try the following questions to assess the plot culmination:

- How are you meeting the issue, challenge, or problem portrayed in the dream?
- Is there a "because factor" in the dream?
- What created the "because factor"?
- How does the plot culmination relate to your present situation?

Part Four: Conclusion (solution or result)

Typically the last part of the dream wraps up the story and conveys the solution or result. Look at your dream for completion. Did it successfully resolve the dilemma, problem, conflict, or issue portrayed in the dream?

All too often your dreams may fail to reach a conclusion. However don't worry, even your unresolved dream dramas offer you a key to understanding the message of the dream.

4. Evaluate the conclusion of your dream using these questions:

- Does the dream have a conclusion?
- Was the dream issue successfully resolved? How was it decided?
- If the issue remained unresolved, identify the reasons.
- Do you feel pleased with the way the dream concluded?
- What does it bring to mind—memories, experiences, people, places, words, ideas?
- What issues need resolving in your life?
- How does the dream ending depict your waking life?
- Does it provide direction about moving your life forward?

▣ 19th c. dreamer— Otto von Bismark

In 1863 Otto von Bismark (1815-1898) had a dream that perhaps laid the foundation for the German Empire in the 20th century. He was riding on a narrow alpine path, with a precipice on one side and rocks on the other.

When the path became so narrow that his horse refused to proceed, Bismarck used his whip to strip away the rocky impasse. The whip grew very long, the rocky wall dropped away, and a broad path appeared in which Prussian troops with banners were moving forward.

In a letter to Emperor William I, Bismark said that the dream gave him confirmation to proceed with his plans to invade Austria.[69]

15

Draw-A-Dream

The force of reason by itself is not powerful enough for getting at truth. –
Basil the Great

Sometimes it is helpful to draw a picture of your dream, especially one that's difficult to describe with words. *Drawing offers you another way to process your dream.* Using a nonverbal approach, you express your dream imaginatively on paper. Crayons, colored markers, plain pencil or pen—it doesn't matter. Simply sketch what you saw in the dream, or some element of it.

Don't be afraid to use stick figures—this isn't an art contest. Using simple figures may help you recall more details. For some examples of dream drawings, see my previous book, *Dream Treasure: Learning the Language of Heaven*[70] (those sketches will assure you that artistic skills are not necessary).

When you finish your drawing, title it and place it where you can look at it for a while. You can use your drawing to help you simply muse or meditate on the dream, without trying to force its meaning. Drawing your dreams can help you find a greater sense of mastery and control over frightful images in the dream.[71]

1. Process your drawing

Use the following questions to help explore your dream for the *treasure* it holds for you:

- What do you see?
- What element feels most important to you? The most intense?
- What does it suggest to you?
- What feelings does it express?
- What feelings does it arouse in you?
- What thoughts or memories does it bring to mind?

2. Imagine it hanging in an art gallery

Try looking at your drawing as if it is hanging in an art gallery. If the dream was such a painting, imagine what the artist has in mind.

- What would the artist be trying to convey?
- What message is this artist trying to communicate?
- In what way is this painting portraying your daily life?

3. Sacramental approach

Draw a picture of the dream or of a key element and bring it with you when you receive the sacraments.

- Kneel before the altar and surrender it to God, asking for His transforming love and grace.
- Pray for clearer understanding or resolution of the dream.

19th c. dreamer— Elias Howe

Elias Howe (1819-1867) worked for years to perfect a lock-stitch sewing machine, but was using a needle threaded through the middle of the shank. In his dream …

He was going to be boiled in a pot by a group of cannibals when he became fascinated by their spears, which had eye-shaped holes near their tips.

When he awoke, instead of drawing his dream he whittled a model of the dream spear with a hole located at the tip, and thereby discovered the detail he required for his sewing machine.[72]

16

Emotional Feeling

Search me, O God, and know my heart; Try me and know my anxious thoughts; and see if there be any hurtful way [way of pain] in me, and lead me in the everlasting way. – Psalm 139:23-24

Dreams are fascinating because they show the truth—the way things really are. They are profoundly honest in exposing our feelings in the narrative we create. *The feeling in our dream can offer an important clue in our dream work process.*

"It is important … to be aware of the feelings elicited by dreams … Finding the feeling that goes with an element (or the element associated with a feeling) adds depth and reality to the experience of your dream."[73]

If we can identify the emotions in a dream, we can notice where we are experiencing these emotions in current everyday life, or when we experienced them at an earlier time. Dreams often use our current prevailing emotion to connect old memories with our most recent experiences.

A few months after Bill Lambier showed up in his dream (see #10 *Biblical Purposes*), Gerald had another dream: "Feeling overwhelming remorse over being a bruiser, I looked for a place to cry it out to God. I knelt by a bed and poured out my heart to God, weeping uncontrollably with extremely deep remorse—a true repentance. The dream showed me God was healing this area of my life. Also I realized the possibility of being the *last* of the Big Bruisers in my family, and I have chosen to bring God's grace into my relationships."

Obviously many types and degrees of emotions can appear. Here are some examples: fear, frightened, embarrassed, terror, anxiety; frustrated, anger, revengeful, enraged, hate; powerless, helplessness, lost, despair; rejected, abandoned, lonely; embarrassed, ashamed, guilt, regret; sadness, sorrow, grief, pain, disappointed, deflated; jealous, envious; joy, delighted, happy; relaxed, surprised, curious, inspired, enthused, exalted, pleased—or just plain numb.

Four emotions commonly found in dreams include apprehension, anger, happiness, and excitement. If you have trouble identifying emotions in your dream, get someone to help you. Ask them, "If this were your dream, what might you be feeling in it?"

1. Identify dream emotions
- What feelings and emotions are being experienced, expressed, dramatized?
- Who felt them?
- What did *you* feel in the dream?
- *How* did you feel about what was happening in the dream?
- Does the behavior of the other characters suggest what feelings they were experiencing?
- Are the feelings given full expression? What restrained them?
- As you awoke, what feelings were still present in you?
- Were you invigorated? Exhausted? Tense? Relaxed?

2. Consider how the dream emotion relates to your everyday life, your current concerns
- Have you ever felt it before? When? Why? Where?
- What situation does this feeling remind you of?
- Where in your everyday life are you feeling this same emotion?
- Is there anything troubling you at the moment that is looking for emotional release?

3. Consider if the dream emotion relates to past experiences
- What people, experiences, places, words, ideas does this emotion bring to mind?
- What memories does this emotion bring to mind?
- Does this emotion relate to something you felt in the past?
- List other experiences where you felt this emotion.
- When did you first experience this feeling?

4. Resolve painful emotion through prayer
- Tell the dream aloud, using the present tense.
- Identify the strongest feeling in the dream as you tell it.
- Ask God, "What memory is connected to the strongest feeling in my dream?" You are looking for the specific memory God wants you to recall.

- Ask God, "What did I believe when this happened?" You are inviting God to show you what needs to be healed in this life experience.
- Ask God, "What is Your truth for me in this memory? What do you want me to know about this experience in my life?"

📧 *20ᵗʰ c. dreamer— Rev. Herman Riffel*

The late Herman Riffel (1917-2009), a Baptist minister, dreamed he was mountain climbing with his family, when the stones gave way under his feet and everyone started sliding toward a chasm below. He suddenly awoke with fear, sensing God was trying to get his attention about a certain family situation.[74]

17

Dream Action

In a "vision in the night" Paul saw a Macedonian man asking him to come to Macedonia and help. Taking action immediately, Paul changed his direction. –
see Acts 16:9, 10

You've been learning how to use a series of questions to draw out the information already visible in the dream and see how it relates to your life." In dream action, the goal is to determine the main action or overall activity in the dream. *Processing your dream actions will help you reflect on how you relate to life.* Are you actively participating in life, or are you merely observing it? Are you running from something?

Because of scene shifts, you may identify several different activities in your dream. In the first scene you may be running; in the next, hiding. You can choose to work with both of the actions, or select only the one that has the most energy for you.

In the early 1980s, Gerald was stalled in his high-tech career and very unhappy with his life. When God decided to redirect his life, He knew how to get around Gerald's logical protestations. Catching him while his conscious mind slept, He sent this dream: "On the 8th floor of an office building, I enter the office of a man named Mr. Sadd. On his desk is a placard that says, 'Forecasting.' I look out the window at a dull, gray day and notice a bluebird on a limb. I feel delighted."

Although Gerald knew little about symbolic language, it was clear that "happiness" would require him to step outside the corporate walls. The initial vision he had for his life—engineering—was completed, and no longer worked for him.

---

u We've identified *dream elements* as all distinguishable features in the dream, including figures, places, actions, and emotions. (For a detailed description of dream elements see #27 *Identify Dream Elements.*)

1. Identify the primary dream activity

To trigger your thinking, we suggest some common activities to look for. Notice if the main dream action involves sleeping, running, walking, climbing, driving, fleeing, flying, crying, hiding, or playing. Other typical actions to look for include: feeding, eating, cooking, looking, searching, hiding, escaping, working, building, fixing, murdering, killing, having sex.

List the actions or activities identified in your dream.

- Which is the primary one?
- Who is doing the action or activity?
- What are *you* doing in the dream?
- Why are *you* doing this activity?

2. Find parallels between the dream activity and your inner or outer life

- What area of your life might this dream be concerned with?
- What life situation are you in that might lead you to choose this dream action?
- What memories, people, experiences, places, words, ideas does this bring to mind?
- In what area of your life are you currently doing this same activity?
- When have you done this activity in the past?
- Why are you doing this activity?

3. Active participant or observer

- What are you actually doing in the dream?
- Do you take a leading role, or are you passively observing what's happening?
- How does this concern your everyday life—work, home, relationships, church, God?

4. Roles played in the dream

Observe the various roles played in your drama. Remember, your roles are not your real self—they represent ways you relate to others.

Identify roles played in the dream:
- What roles can you recognize in the dream?
- Is anyone wearing a uniform?
- What role are *you* playing? Why are you playing this role?
- What role did the principal character play?

Find parallels between dream roles and your outer life:
- What memories, people, experiences, places, words, or ideas does this role bring to mind?
- Do you like the role you're playing in the dream?
- In what area of your life are you playing this role now?
- How do you currently *feel* about playing this role in life?
- Is this a role that you chose? Are forced to play? Feel at home with? Is habitual to you?

5. Other types of movement

Every type of movement in our dreams shows us something: blowing wind, rushing water, rising flood waters, tsunami, hurricane, tidal wave, swirling clouds, fire, growing plants, waving grain, lightning, shooting stars. Consider any movement to be a metaphor, depicting some reality in your life. To process dream movement, ask the following questions:
- What are the characteristics and positive or negative purposes of this movement?
- What memories, people, experiences, places, words, or ideas does this movement bring to mind?
- Is this movement concerned with your current situation, inner life, or something in the future?

6. Physical sensations

Identify any physical sensations you experienced in the dream: physical pain, tired, exhausted, chilled, frozen, sweating, at ease, hungry, satisfied, sexual arousal. Describe the sensation you felt.

- What positive or negative purpose does this sensation serve?
- What memories, people, experiences, places, words, or ideas does this sensation bring to mind?
- What life situation are you in that might lead you to choose this sensation in your dream?

▤ 4ᵗʰ c. dreamer— Emperor Constantine

The first Christian emperor, Constantine (272-337 AD), on the night before the liberation of Rome in 312, received battle instructions in a dream.

He was told to paint the Christian monogram (the sign of the cross) on his troops' shields as a safeguard against his enemies. He passed this command on to his troops before his attack, which led to victory against Maxentius in the historic Battle of the Milvian Bridge.

Constantine then ended the persecution of Christians, converted to Christianity, and made it the official religion of the Roman empire.[75]

18

Dream Ego Figure

Dreams help us realize every part of our potential and bring us into harmony with God, others, and ourselves. – Rev. Herman Riffel[76]

One of our key dream figures portrays the ego: the part of us we refer to as "I" in the daytime. Although it's not literally me, the ego figure represents my conscious awareness, my present point of view. Usually it looks exactly like me.

By observing the attitudes and feelings our dream ego figure carries and how it makes choices, we get an amazing perspective on how we behave in various situations in our daily life. It also helps us to connect our daytime choices (decisions of our waking ego) with what's going on within our heart. Sometimes our dream ego figure knows something we do not.

We process our dream ego figure by examining what it's doing and feeling in the dream, and comparing that to what we're doing in our waking hours.[77] In his bluebird dream (#17 *Dream Action*), Gerald realized that personal contentment could not be found inside the corporation—he would have to go outside the office walls to find his true life.

As he pondered what to do, God sent Gerald an extremely powerful dream: "Flood waters are lapping at my doorstep. An office colleague says we must leave immediately. I think we should go to the second floor to wait out the flood. When the others leave, I head upstairs. I begin to feel concerned about the flood waters, but I am uncomfortable leaving without my favorite leather jacket. A woman helps me find my jacket in a dresser drawer. I put on the jacket and step outside."

Discussing his dream with spiritually astute friends, Gerald realized the actions of his dream ego figure depicted exactly what he was doing in his career in the face of threat—trying to wait it out. He realized that he needed to take action immediately. Three days later, he decided to take a leave of absence from his job. We sold our house, wandered the USA for a while in a camper trailer, then traveled to Europe and Israel.

Although he could no longer live in the comfortable, seemingly secure corporate world, Gerald was unable to leave it until the dream energized him. Profoundly changed inside, he began to listen more intentionally to the voice of God in his dreams.

1. What is the dream ego figure doing?

List the things your dream ego did: how it acted, what it said, what it chose, how it responded to the situation. You may have many actions to list or only a few.

- List the actions of your dream ego figure.
- What attitudes does the ego figure display?
- What is the ego figure feeling?
- What choices did it make?
- How did it respond to the situation it was facing?
- Are you pleased with its choices and behaviors?
- If not, how would you change it?

2. Find parallels between behavior of dream ego figure and your choices in waking life

- What memories, people, experiences, places, words, or ideas do the actions of the dream ego figure bring to mind?
- How do the actions, attitudes and feelings of the dream ego compare to those of your waking ego?
- In what area of your life are you behaving like your dream ego figure?
- What do you think God is trying to make you aware of through this dream?

▤ 19th c. dreamer—Father Bosco (Giovanni Bosco)

St. John Bosco (Giovanni Bosco, 1815–1888) became a priest and founded the Salesian order (monks who care for homeless children) because God spoke to him in his dreams in his youth.

When Pope Pius IX heard of Father Bosco's dreams, he ordered him to record it for the benefit of his Salesian order.

At age nine, he dreamed that a luminous man in a white cloak told him he must win over boys by kindness, not by the violent punching behavior of the first part of his dream.

In another dream, Bosco was with wild animals, when a woman in a brilliant, sparkly garment showed him some wild animals, which turned into lambs as he watched. She told Bosco that would be his life's work.

As a teen, Bosco had several more dreams that encouraged him to care for abandoned youth. Later he dreamed again that he was in a group of animals when the shepherdess again appeared and signaled him to follow her. As they journeyed along, many of the animals turned into lambs. Eventually some of the lambs turned into shepherds.[78]

19

Dream Words

In Gibeon the Lord appeared to Solomon in a dream at night, and God said, 'Ask what you wish me to give you.' – 1 Kings 3:5

Spoken words—even thoughts—are dream elements we can process in our quest to understand the message in our dream. A complete sentence, clearly spoken or thought in the dream, we call a key statement. *It offers us a simple clue in our discovery process.*

Our challenge is to make a connection between what is happening in everyday life and the words or thoughts in our dreams. We look for parallels between that word, thought, or key statement and our outer or inner life.

After Gerald escaped the corporate world, we settled into a rural Michigan area and worked for a nonprofit organization. After his nerves calmed, Gerald considered what was next for his life. He faced a crisis: how could he earn a living? He was lost—all he knew was corporate life.

One night God sent him a dream: "Comedian Bill Cosby asked me to pronounce this sentence: 'Everyone in New England has a favorite book.' I explained that the meaning would change, depending which words were emphasized. I read the sentence several times, emphasizing first one word, then another, to change its meaning. Amazed, Cosby said three things in my right ear: 'Rhodes Scholar,' 'Engineering is done,' and … (I couldn't recall)."

Cosby (a shadow figure) helped Gerald see that he also could view his potential work from a variety of perspectives—he had much more capability than he ever imagined while stuck in his corporate role. As his inner image began to change, he launched a new career as a freelance business writer (despite no training in writing or journalism, he hadn't studied English since they wrote the textbook—oh, and he couldn't type). Where did the faith come from to do that? From the words in his dream!

1. Identify any words, thoughts, phrases, or statements in the dream

- List the words, phrases, or key statements spoken or thought.
- Does any particular statement or word have more intensity than the others?
- Who says or thinks it?
- What are *you* saying or thinking?

2. Find parallels between words in the dream and your outer life or inner world

- What memories, people, experiences, places, words, ideas do the words/thoughts bring to mind?
- Where in your life are you currently thinking or saying something similar?
- How do the words, thoughts or key statement relate to what is going on in your life?
- What life situation are you in that might lead you to say these words in your dream?
- How do you currently *feel* about these words?
- Where did you learn to *think* that particular thought or say those words?
- What area of your life do you think this dream is concerned with?

8th c. dreamer—Bishop Aubert

St. Aubert, 8th century bishop of the French town of Avranches, dreamed the archangel Michael ordered him to build a chapel. He founded the now-famous Mont-St-Michel off the coast of Normandy. This abbey (accessible by land today only at low tide) has been a sanctuary for pilgrims, and popular tourist destination, for more than a thousand years.[79]

20

Dream Intensity

When working with a dream, go where the energy takes you, to the symbolic imagery that contains the greatest amount of energy for you.[80] *– Dr. Robert A. Johnson*

Because we are made in the image of God, deep within us we contain immense energy. While we sleep, images and symbols in our dreams can transform this vital energy in a way that re-energizes us for everyday living. Because God is the source of all energy, *our dreams often contain divine energy,* capable of restoring our soul and renewing us in our entire being.

Dreams can provide us spiritual and psychological liveliness we never knew existed. Divine energy can be imparted to us in a dream, because it contains a *living* Word—in picture form—from God. This energy can transform the way we see ourselves and the world around us.

Our dreams can bring together the fractured pieces of our conflicted, divided heart. They can help us complete an unfinished project or provide additional enthusiasm to tackle new activities. Dreams can release our creativity—discoveries and inventions sometimes come through dreams.

Transformative power of the dream

Some dream symbols offer transformation, precisely because of the divine energy embedded in them. Charged with intense energy, these symbols arouse strong feelings—awe, terror, delight, deep peace—which linger long after we awake. They capture our emotional attention with an intensity that forces our energy into paths that can cause big changes in our lives.

Following is a dream whose power had escaped Gerald for many years until he revisited it recently while I was writing this book: "I was telling a group of people on a street corner how great God is, how He is full of grace and mercy, and how He has touched my life so deeply. The more I shared, the more enthusiastic I became.

My voice carried out some distance as more people began listening to me. *Life* was in me and flowing out of me as I simply shared the goodness of God and what He has done for me. People were being touched by me and what I was saying."

As Gerald shared this dream with me, suddenly he felt a tremendous influx of divine energy, as the meaning of the dream struck him. God reminded him that this dream was still full of divine life after 13 years, and continues to hold transformative power for him.

If we try to force an interpretation of a dream analytically, the symbols can lose their intensity: their power to impact our life drains away. Rather than try to obtain an arbitrary interpretation of a dream symbol, it's better to pay attention to its vitality and vividness. In dream work, the intensity of images is more significant than their precision and clarity.

> If we oversimplify dream interpretation or try to reduce our dreams to pat meanings, their value and vitality will elude us. (Morton Kelsey)[81]

The more intense the symbols, the more important the dream message is. When choosing a dream or dream element to work with, I have learned to select the most highly charged image, one that brings up a surge of energy in me.

1. Rate the intensity

To process the dream energy, practice rating its intensity.

- Using a scale of 0 (none) to 10 (maximum), how intense is this dream?
- Which dream element holds the most energy for you?
- Which dream element *feels* the most compelling?

2. Sketch a dream element

- Sketch a picture of this dream element, allowing yourself to feel its energy.
- What personal recollections does this element bring to mind?
- Note any surge of energy in you.

▤ 20th c. dreamer—Acrobat Tito Gaona

Tito Gaona, a famous acrobat, said that he sometimes discovered new acrobatic tricks while dreaming at night. Next day he would try to master the trick on the wires.

His original "double forward somersault with a double full twist at the same time" came to him in a dream; it had never been done before.[82]

Dear King Solomon,

I have a dream for you, but first I want to explain how this one goes down. Usually I tell the dream story in symbolic form, making folks dig a little to understand the symbols and extract the meaning of the message I'm delivering to them. This one's a little different.

This time I'm participating directly in the dream, and I invite you to do the same. Also (a bit out of the ordinary) I'm going to ask you to respond *right in the dream*, instead of later in your dream journal. It'll be fun, just the two of us having a conversation right in the dream.

In Gibeon the Lord appeared to Solomon in a dream at night; and God said, "Ask what you wish Me to give you."

Then Solomon said, "You have shown great lovingkindness to Your servant David my father, … Now, O Lord my God, You have made Your servant king in place of my father David, yet I am but a little child … So give Your servant an understanding heart to judge Your people to discern between good and evil."

God said to him, "Because you have asked … for yourself discernment to understand justice, behold, I have done according to your words. Behold, I have given you a wise and discerning heart, so that there has been no one like you before you, nor shall one like you arise after you." (1 Kings 3:5-12)

Sincerely yours,

Yahweh, Giver of Wisdom

Part Four

Non-Interpretive Strategies

Many dreams cannot be opened up intellectually or rationally; we must engage them using our intuitive and imaginative faculties. Our right-brain faculties such as intuition and imagination can take us out of our analytical mindset and offer us alternative ways to work with dreams.

Aware of the importance of the inner world, *Jesus Christ tried to get people to embrace faith in their hearts*, not just the rationality of their conscious minds. Jesus urged people to get out of their heads and into their hearts. He deliberately used parables, similes, and metaphors to help them skirt around the conscious mind and directly connect to the unconscious. As David Benner says, "God is far too big for our engagement with Him or response to Him to be adequately contained within consciousness."[83]

In Part Four, I describe non-interpretative strategies that can help you to get out of your head and into your heart. You will notice that these techniques often overlap, because they use both our intuitive and imaginative capabilities.

Dream work principles
☆ Dream meditation offers a way to bring our dreams to the One who gave them to us.
☆ Created by God, our imagination is a powerful source of healing and revelation in unlocking the mystery of dreams.

☆ Focusing attention on questions the dream raises helps us establish a dialogue with its Divine Source.

☆ An imaginative, conversational encounter with a dream figure can be a powerful resource in dream work.

☆ Nightmares are an invitation to come to our Heavenly Father for healing.

☆ A dream sharing group offers a place to receive support, gather intuitive feedback, and benefit from the imaginative input of others.

21

Meditative Strategies

Meditate in your heart upon your bed, and be still. – Psalm 4:4

Scripture tells us to meditate on what God says to us. The word *meditation* comes from a Hebrew word meaning "to muse, ponder, imagine." The Old Testament Israelis were instructed to meditate on the words the Lord had given them, indicating that this was the way to success (Josh 1:8).

Dream author Morton Kelsey said, "We can find few better ways of coming into contact with the Holy Spirit than by writing down our dreams and meditating upon them and bringing them before the One who gave them to us."[84]

Quiet yourself

Meditative Strategies ask us to become still inside, to push aside our argumentative brain box, rather than trying to grasp a dream's meaning with our intellect. We do something to take our thoughts away from life in the fast lane. Perhaps we listen to soft, contemplative music, sift through an art book, enjoy the beauty of nature, or sing softly in the Spirit—anything that promotes a peaceful, reflective atmosphere.

When you put your everyday worries and concerns aside and muse or meditate on your dream images, you gain new strength and peace. You may sense a felt connection between your outer conscious world and your inner disquieted world, or even sense God. Because symbolic images are linked to energy deep within, when the connection is made, you'll feel sparks fly.

Apply your heart

To meditate on our dreams, we must apply our heart, i.e., tune into the flow coming from our heart—pictures, images and symbols. But most of us don't have much experience with flowing pictures and thoughts arising from our deep heart. Unless we are poets or song writers, we're more comfortable with the linear reasoning of our left brain.

If we don't tune into our hearts, we might make mistakes. Solomon deliberately tells us not to look to our analytical reasoning, but to use our hearts: "Make your ear attentive to wisdom, incline your heart [stretch your heart out] to understanding" (Prov 2:2).

Use your intuition

I believe intuition is key in our search for the hidden treasure embedded in our dreams. Nearly all of us are totally lost with our right-brain capacities—symbolic thinking, imagination, intuition, and art appreciation—that bring us into contact with our heart. However, our intuitive and imaginative abilities are potent resources in unlocking the mystery of our dreams.

A dictionary says that *intuition* "is the direct perception of truth, independent of any reasoning process."[85] When we have a "hunch" or a premonition that comes seemingly out of nowhere, from somewhere deep inside, that's intuition at work. It is spiritual perception that bubbles up from within. Maybe it seems like a soundless voice or a wordless monitor that urges, moves, confirms, or constrains us in some way.[86]

Rabbi Moses Maimonides, the highly influential medieval Jewish philosopher and physician, said, "the source of our knowledge of God is the inner eye, 'the eye of the heart,' a medieval name for intuition."[87] We perceive or see God through the eyes of the heart, not our intellect.

1. Muse on a dream or dream image

Choose a dream or dream image to work with. Simply relate to it, savoring it as you do with some memorable experience in your life.

- "Hold the dream in a sacred reverie."[88]
- Re-experience it and savor the dream or image.
- Walk around inside a dream and "make it your friend," taking it into your heart.[89]
- Allow it to show you what you most need to focus attention on, what you need to ponder.

2. Read your dream aloud in the present tense

Another idea is to read your dream as if it were a meditation or a Scripture reading.

- Slowly read the dream aloud, savoring each word picture.
- What do you sense in your soul as you read?
- Tune into any eruptions or in-breakings of the Holy Spirit.[90]
- Note how it brings you closer to God, Your Father.

3. Contemplate or meditate on a dream or its image

Contemplating or meditating on a dream goes a step further than simply musing on it. Intentionally fixing your attention on it sets up an energy flow between your heart and conscious mind.[91]

- Select a dream image; intentionally fix your attention on it.
- Observe or study it, thinking deeply about it.
- Reflect on the psychological & spiritual meaning it might offer.
- Tune into the flow of your heart, allowing the still, small voice of your heart to speak to you.
- Note any spontaneous images or thoughts that appear.
- Be sensitive to any felt connection between the image and your soul or spirit.
- How might it connect you to God? To yourself? To others?

4. Listening prayer

In listening prayer, you are intentionally opening your inner self to God and inviting Him to step into your dream.

- Enter the Lord's presence through prayer and invite Him to be with you in your dream.
- Ask God to show you what He wants you to know.
- Tune into the flow of your heart, allowing God to show you something.
- Allow the pictures to spontaneously move in response to the Holy Spirit.
- Stay tuned in to the Lord—see, hear, sense what He does.
- When finished, ask, "What is God trying to show me?"
- What does this experience mean to you?

5. View dream as a parable—"It is as if … ."

Jesus' words were designed to reach hearts, not intellects. As Kelsey says, "If we should complain that He should speak more clearly, it is helpful to remember that Jesus spoke His deepest truths of salvation in the language of metaphor, simile, and parable."[92] When words connect to your heart, you experience an intuitive knowing or witness to the truth of something.

I speak to them in parables because, while seeing they do not see, and while hearing they do not hear, nor do they understand (Matt 13:13).

A useful approach is to consider your dream *as if it were a parable.* Like parables, dreams draw you into the story until suddenly their message is quite obvious and often surprisingly simple.[93] Parables are not direct statements you can grasp with your conscious ego; they are short stories designed to teach some truth. They convey meaning indirectly by use of comparison or analogy.

- When you consider your dream as a parable, you compare the dream with something else.
- Start by saying, "It is as if … " or "It is as though … "
- Be aware of spontaneous thoughts or that light upon your mind.[94]
- Try to discern the dream's overall theme or question, rather than its one true meaning.
- What kind of life situation might you be in that would lead you to choose just that story?
- Attempt to find spiritual connections and deeper meaning in its images.
- What does it show about your fate or the process of your growth?
- When finished, ask, "What new insights or perspectives about my dream do I have?"

📄 19th c. dreamer—Albert Einstein

Albert Einstein (1879-1955) experienced an adolescent dream in which he achieved the speed of light and saw stars change into amazing patterns and colors. Reflecting on this dream through the years led him to propose his famous theory of relativity.

22

Imaginative Strategies

Rabbi Moses Maimonides (12ᵗʰ C) viewed dreams as a kind of prophecy: "The action of the imaginative faculty during sleep is the same as at the time when it receives a prophecy."[95]

According to Robert Johnson,[v] dreams and visions are the first of the two great channels of communication from the deep heart; the second is the imagination.[96] *Created by God, our imagination is a powerful source of healing and revelation in dream work.* Einstein famously said: "Imagination is more important than knowledge."[97]

Imagination is the ability to conceptualize, or to construct mental images of, what is not actually present to our senses. This capacity to form pictures in our heads is a deeply creative faculty. Our challenge is to learn how to use our God-given imagination and place it in the service of the Holy Spirit in our dream work.

About the imagination

Our imagination is an inner eye, part of our intuitive capability that allows us to see the spiritual world. It enables us to observe the invisible arena we can't see with the natural, physical eye. In cooperation with our spirit, our imagination can create pictures of what the Holy Spirit reveals to us.

The Bible says to "prepare your minds for action" (1 Pet 1:13). The Greek word for mind, *dianoia*, includes the imaginative aspect of the mind. As the generating and creating power of the mind, the imagination is either a tool for faith or for unbelief. A doubting, fearful imagination works from the outer, soulish realm, and is open to attack from the enemy. But a faith-filled, spiritual imagination works from our renewed spirit.

---

v Robert A. Johnson (1921–) is a noted depth psychologist, author, and lecturer on wholeness and dream work.

Activate the imaginative process

The imaginative strategies that follow are helpful in unlocking the mystery of our dreams To activate your imaginative capabilities, you consciously kick-start the process, then allow it to continue without ego control or direction. Let it flow spontaneously and show you something from your heart.

As you try an imaginative approach, we recommend that you use a light touch. Keep a playful spirit. Then share your experiences with spiritually-attuned friends.

1. Imagine your dream belongs to another

One strategy is to pretend that your dream belongs to someone else, perhaps a close friend or even a lesser-known acquaintance. This approach has the effect of putting the dream outside you objectively. Because it relieves any pressure to get it right, this may help free your imaginative capacities.

- Read your dream aloud, but read it *as if it were not yours.*
- Ask, "If this dream were so-and-so's, what might it be saying to them?"
- Ask, "Why do they need this dream story"?
- Ask, "What kind of life situation might they be in that would bring them this dream?"

2. Imagine your dream as if it were a play or a movie

Because the dream comes from an unknown area within you, it's helpful to relate to it as if it were something totally outside of you.

- Approach your dream as if it were a theater play or a movie.
- Observe its beginning, notice the unfolding of the situation, follow development of the action, and understand its conclusion.
- What type of movie is it: adventure, mystery, comedy, romance, thriller?
- What feelings & human situations is it depicting?
- What message is it giving?
- In what way does this movie correspond to your daily life; how does it differ?

3. Role playing: "What part of me is that? What is it saying?"

Dreams can help you accept ownership of your own issues instead of projecting them onto others or blaming others. Assume the various parts of the dream are facets of your total self—opposing and inconsistent sides. Spontaneously role play each element, acting and creating a dialogue with the other parts. Allow it to show you what it feels like, and what it means, to be that part.

Role playing each part enables you to actually experience the feelings associated with your conflicts, instead of merely talking about them in a detached fashion.[98] It helps you see how you are responding to life and where you might need to make changes. You perceive more clearly your way of being in the world and perhaps expose some ways you're avoiding your life.

- Bring the dream back to life by re-telling it in the present tense.
- Role play each part—imagine an element as a part of yourself.
- Write out what each part is saying.
- Connect each part to your inner life.
- What part of you feels or thinks that way?
- What part of you is behaving like that?

4. Re-enter a dream

Using your God-given imagination, you can re-enter a disturbing dream to explore some aspect or element and perhaps resolve the pain in it. This approach offers you a way to draw upon the positive energy in a dream or find a creative solution to a troubling problem. You may be able to complete an unfinished dream, rewrite an unsatisfactory ending, release negative energy, or work through a traumatic experience.

As God's child, you can invite the Son of God, Jesus Christ, to come with you as you re-enter your dream, and watch to see what He might do or say.

- Pray, inviting the Lord to accompany you as you re-enter the dream.
- Using your imagination, re-enter dream and observe the free flow of imagery with your mind's eye.

- Look around in the dream and see if you can sense the presence of Jesus or other godly figures with you.
- Pay attention to what you hear, see, or sense Him doing.
- Allow Jesus to resolve the pain, show you something you didn't know, or perhaps give you a creative solution to a troubling problem.
- Did you experience some type of shift in your awareness—an "*Aha!*"?

5. Turn and face it

This technique draws upon your ability to make choices for yourself when you are increasingly aware of something troubling you. In your dream, if you become aware that you are running from something, or sense something is following you, decide to turn and face it. Find out what you are running from.

- Stop running away or hiding.
- Turn around and face it; perhaps reach out and touch the thing you're afraid of.
- Ask, "Who are you, and what do you want from me?"
- Did you experience some type of shift in your awareness—an "*Aha!*"?

6. Alter the dream

Bring the dream back to life and re-enter it. Imagine yourself in the dream and continue it as a fantasy or a daydream. See if you can change it in some way, perhaps to find a more satisfying conclusion.

It's important to be aware of any suppressed anger or hostility in your dream. In your imagination, give full expression to your anger or hostility: let it out, take it to God.

Choose a dream that did not reach a satisfactory conclusion, or one in which you are not pleased with the choices you made in it.

- Re-enter the dream imaginatively, immersing yourself in it.
- Alter the dream in any way you like.
- Experiment with it, play with it, until you are satisfied with the result.

7. Write a story

Writing a story based on a dream offers another playful way to relate to a dream and its imagery. Immerse yourself in the dream, and then allow its characters or images to spontaneously change or move forward in time. When finished, you will have created a new story, perhaps changing the end of the dream in a more positive, insightful way.[99]

- Re-enter the dream, immersing yourself in it.
- Spontaneously begin to rewrite the dream, making better choices or a more life-enhancing ending.
- Do you feel satisfied with your new story?
- Did you release negative energy or work through a traumatic experience as you wrote?
- Did you experience a shift in your awareness—an *"Aha!"*?

🖻 20ᵗʰ c. dreamer—David Parkinson

In 1940 a Bell Labs engineer, Dr. David A. Parkinson, was working on the design for an automatic level recorder to improve accuracy of telephone transmission measurements. He had a dream:

In a gun pit with an antiaircraft crew, Parkinson noticed that one of the guns successfully downed an airplane with every shot. When a crew member showed him the exposed end of the gun, he was amazed to see the control potentiometer of his level recorder attached there.

The first all-electric antiaircraft gun director evolved from research based on his dream. It was also the forerunner of later, more sophisticated, antiballistic missile guidance systems.[100]

23

Dream Questions

God said to him, "Because you ... have asked for yourself discernment to understand justice, behold I have done according to your words." Then Solomon awoke and behold it was a dream. – 1 Kings 3:5-15

Most of us like to approach a dream as if it should give us answers, advice or prophetic revelation. Perhaps we'll get more from our dreams if, instead of searching for answers, we look at the questions invoked by the dream. *Focusing our attention on what questions the dream raises helps us establish a dialogue with its Divine Source.*

Usually dreams don't provide direct answers or tell us exactly what to do. Instead they raise questions, present alternatives, and suggest possibilities, encouraging us to make further inquiry.[101]

1. Reflect on questions offered by your dream

In this technique, we brainstorm a list of questions the dream might be asking us, and then we reflect on one or two of the questions using our journal.

- List questions or invitations your dream might be offering you.
- Choose a compelling question or invitation to reflect on.
- Spontaneously write your response to the question or invitation.
- Reflect on how your response to the question or invitation will influence your daily life.
- Did you experience a shift in your awareness—an *"Aha!"*?

2. What questions do you have for your dream?

In this technique we brainstorm a list of questions that we have for the dream. Try asking relational and functional questions, rather than informative ones: Why is this dream coming to me now? Why am I behaving like this? Then choose a question to explore.

- Brainstorm a list of questions you have for your dream.
- Select a question and spontaneously write a response to it.
- Use the question to kick off an imaginative conversation with God.
- Note any shift in your awareness—an "*Aha!*"

🖅 *14ᵗʰ c. dreamer—Jacobo Dante*

After the death of Dante, the famous poet, his son Jacobo searched for months unsuccessfully for the last 13 cantos of Dante's Paradise.

Then Dante appeared in Jacobo's dream and talked with his son. With a radiant face and clothed in white, Dante assured his son—who questioned the life hereafter—that he continued to exist.

When asked about the missing cantos, Dante led Jacobo to a room Dante often slept in, touched a wall and said, "What you have sought for so much is here."

When he woke up, Jacobo went to the bedroom of the house where his father died. Lifting a mat on the wall, he discovered a small window, and there, covered in mold, were the missing cantos.[102]

24

Dream Dialogue

*Often when the body is quiet, and at rest and asleep, man moves inwardly ...
and the soul ... imagines and beholds things above the earth, and often even
holds converse with the saints and angels who are above earthly and bodily
existence.*[103] *– Athanasius*[w]

King Solomon conversed with God in a dream, even receiving his
famous divine wisdom in the dream. St. Thomas Aquinas had a discussion with St. Peter and St. Paul in his dream, giving Aquinas help with
his writing. Mother Teresa encountered St. Peter at the gates of heaven, in
a dream that provided her the direction and energy for her ministry.

Exercising our God-given gift of imagination, we also can converse
with a figure from our dreams. My personal experience verifies what other
Christian dream experts say: *An imaginative conversational encounter with
our dream figures can be a powerful resource for drawing out the meaning of
the dream and resolving conflicts.*

Christian psychologist David Benner says that dialogue with a dream
symbol in our imagination can still be guided by God. Our dream figures
are a gift from God to bless us. We should actively work to receive the
gift—wrestle with these figures like Jacob did, if necessary.[104]

Keep to the right

Some more rational and analytical approaches demand the use of our
left–brain functions. Other techniques require us to utilize the creative
side of our minds, our imaginative capability.

When we dialogue with dream figures, we use our imaginative and
intuitive capacities to kick start a conversation with a dream figure. This
slides us out from underneath rational control and into the non-rational
realm to open ourselves to new awareness.

---

w Early Church Father, Bishop Athanasius (4th C.), was a brilliant thinker whose writings were
considered to be authoritative by Catholic, Protestant, and Orthodox theologians. Morton
Kelsey says he laid the foundation for much subsequent Christian thinking.

Talk with ourselves

Dialoguing with our dream figures is much the same as daydreaming, or having a conversation with ourselves. Similar to the way we sometimes reflect aloud to ourselves, we can dialogue with our dream symbols. Each dream character represents a facet of ourselves. In our imagination we strike up a conversation with these figures, and ask them who they are or what they mean.

Note: This is *not* talking to spirit guides or some demonic reality. In the Christian use of dialogue we are engaging in a two-way conversation between our dream figure and our self.

We can disagree with what the dream figure says, and we can even challenge it—Peter did that in his visionary experience at Joppa (Acts 10:9-16). We can do this because we remain conscious and can choose our response.[105]

Choose a dream figure for dialogue

In a playful way, you personify in your mind who or what you want to converse with. You can dialogue with other people, events in your life, your career, dream images, a famous person, your body, etc. Unless it comes easily, you don't need to develop a clear image of the figure. Often just holding the idea of the dream is sufficient.

1. Prepare for dialogue

- Find a quiet place; bring paper and pen, or a recorder.
- Think of several questions you want to ask the dream figure.
- Sit back, close your eyes, let your self become quiet.
- Welcome the presence of the Lord, asking for His guidance.

2. Converse with dream figure

- Gradually open yourself to the dream and the dream figure, as if the dream is happening all over again.
- With your imagination, replay the dream scene where the dream figure appeared.
- Let your mind come into contact with the dream figure.
- Don't try to direct your thoughts, just feel what is there. Greet who it is.
- Ask a question to get the relationship started (in your imagination, picture yourself asking the question to your dream figure).

- Inquire about what they are doing, why they appeared in your dream, what they represent of yourself, what they have brought you.
- Record the response the figure seems to be giving you, but keep your attention focused inward.

3. Conclude and ponder

- When you sense the conversation is coming to an end, you might want to ask if there is anything else the figure wants to say to you.
- Draw the conversation to a close, sit back, and record how you felt as you dialogued.
- Reflect on your experience, noting any impressions, insights or feelings.
- Later, reread it. You may discover something new or find a shift in some attitude.

🖹 13ᵗʰ c. dreamer—Thomas Aquinas

When Thomas Aquinas (1225-1274)* was writing his *Summa Theologica*, he struggled to complete a certain theological passage. Then he dreamed: In a dialogue with St. Peter and St. Paul, Aquinas was instructed on how to handle this difficult theological part of his writing. Next morning he was able to dictate the passage easily. When questioned about it by his surprised scribe, Aquinas explained that his dream showed him how to write it.[106]

* Thomas Aquinas, 13th century theologian, de-emphasized the supernatural dimension, discounting the Bible, Early Church Fathers, and his own dream experiences. Although he changed his views before he died, he turned much of the church away from valuing dreams.

Dear Baker Bob,

You know, recently I sent your colleague, Franklin, the butler, a dream that gave him his ticket out of the gated community you guys have been living in courtesy of the Pharaoh. Franklin was rightly pleased with that little communication from me. He quickly picked up on his old techniques and made some pretty decent Merlot for the Pharaoh. It's good to be in favor with the king.

But, Bob, not all dreams are the same. I have a rather large repertoire of them I can draw from, and the letter I'm sending you is ... ahh ... it's a little delicate ... well, you see, a baker is different from a cupbearer, and I have some other type of news for you. Here's how it's gonna go down:

The baker dreamed of three white baskets stacked on his head, filled with baked goods for Pharaoh. However, the birds got there first and ate the Pharaoh's favorite cinnamon rolls (based on Gen 40:16-17).

Sincerely,

Yahweh, Maker of Bread of Life

25

Nightmares and Recurrent Motifs

I saw a dream and it made me fearful; and these ... visions ... kept alarming me. – Daniel 4:5

requently I am asked if nightmares are caused by the enemy, Satan. In my experience, recurring, severe nightmares are a signal that we have unhealed areas in our hearts. These troubling dreams have a positive intention, alerting us to the need to become more aware of something going on in our waking life. *I view nightmares as an invitation to come to our Heavenly Father for healing.*

Some experts suggest that significant dreams can be identified simply because they *feel* important and are so unforgettable.[107] Nightmares and repetitive dream motifs are especially memorable. It has been said that there is no such thing as a "bad dream"—only dreams that take a dramatically negative form in order to grab our attention.

Highly-charged dreams are one way God gets our attention. Elihu, Job's advisor, asserts that God speaks to us in dreams—even multiple times on the same subject—trying to get our attention. Failing this, the Almighty may turn up the heat, offering us frightening dreams or nightmares that jolt us into awareness (Job 33:14-22).

Nightmares & trauma dreams

In a nightmare, we are in some kind of danger or observing a horrible event. Often paralyzed by fear or shock, we feel lost, helpless, manipulated by something beyond our control. We wake up terrified. Usually the experience is not completed in the dream, suggesting we have unresolved issues in our lives.

Nightmares may be revealing our torments or replaying traumatic experiences we have not processed. Veterans often relive their war experiences this way. Other factors such as drugs, illness, or stress may also contribute to nightmares.

Some especially traumatic dreams cause the dreamer to repeatedly re-live a life-threatening experience such as war, natural catastrophe, accidents, abuse, or violence. Packed with emotional energy, they cause the dreamer to re-experience the traumatic event until, hopefully, it is integrated into conscious awareness. Evidence suggests dreaming about stressful life events promotes healing from them.[108] Research also shows that dreams representing traumatic events convey how the dreamer feels relative to the trauma, including helplessness, terror, and grief.[109]

What causes nightmares?

Since understanding a problem is the first step toward a solution, here are some suggested causes of nightmares:

- Childhood fear: being lost or abandoned; loss of a parent; attack by a parent or a stranger.
- Some terrifying event: vicious attack such as rape or attempted murder; natural disaster like flood, forest fire, or earthquake; trauma from military combat or life-shattering experiences.
- Adult anxiety associated with feelings about our self-esteem, personal security, major change or inner growth: these fears often involve our work, home, and relationships.
- Unconscious memories of intense emotions, e.g., a child being left in a hospital without mother.
- Precognition of fateful events.
- Serious physical illness; impending death.

Repeated dream themes

We need to pay special attention when a dream motif keeps reappearing, because usually it is flagging its importance to us. Recurring themes indicate we have something happening in us that wants to be expressed or requests attention—it needs to be made conscious and incorporated into our everyday life. Multiple dreams in one night may all be calling attention to the same issue—even though they have different imagery and story lines.

The recurrent dream is particularly helpful in healing deep personal psycho-spiritual injuries and resolving individual emotional traumas.[110]

Repetition also may occur because we failed to receive and act on the dream's message the first time it came. According to Elihu's advice to Job, God first tries to get our attention by a "still small voice"; if this fails, we are treated to troubling dreams or nightmares.

Some dreams may be repeated because they are prophetic or visionary, vital to God's greater purposes. Other dreams may repeat variations of a theme, because God is patient and waits until we get it. In Genesis 41, repeating the dream twice to Pharaoh meant that the matter was determined by God, who would quickly accomplish it. If we should dream the same dream three times in one night, it likely contains a direct and powerful message from God.

1. Ways to work with troubling dreams

- View nightmare as an invitation to come to your Heavenly Father for healing and deliverance.
- Read dream aloud, allowing yourself to feel again the emotions expressed in it.
- Look for parallels between dream and your thoughts or feelings in the past: see if you can make a *felt* connection to an unresolved trauma.
- Sacramental approach: a) take a written description of the dream or a drawing of it when you receive the sacraments; b) kneel before the altar and surrender the dream to God for His transforming love and grace.
- Next time you experience this theme, make a decision to *turn and face* the thing you fear (#22 *Imaginative Strategies*).
- Meditational prayer: Go to Jesus and invite Him to be with you in your dream. Use your imagination to watch and see what He will do (#21 *Meditative Strategies*).

2. Rewrite a dream from childhood

One way to resolve a troubling dream from childhood is to rewrite it as if it were a life story or a fairy tale. Begin writing with the famous line, "Once upon a time," then write a story around the issue in the dream. But it's your story, so make the issue that's troubling you appear in a positive light.

Finish your story with a new ending that solves the problem and leaves you with pleasant memories (see also #22, *Imaginative Strategies*).

3. Imagery Rehearsal Technique (IRT)[111]

Imagery Rehearsal Technique (IRT) is a cognitive technique that does not require us to re-experience or re-enter a painful dream. IRT is based on the premise that we can choose our attitudes toward our traumatic dream. We consciously decide how we want to change our dream, cognitively establish new imagery for our dream, and then rehearse the changed drama. IRT seems to work better with older nightmares than with more recent ones.

Try this approach:
- Verbally tell your dream to someone.
- Determine how you would like to change the dream narrative, and make it into a new story.
- What one change do you want to make in the dream?
- Retell the dream with the one change, replacing whatever part you choose.
- Recite this new dream narrative several times a day (not the old nightmare).
- Continue doing this until the traumatic content is gone.

▭ 4th c. dreamer—St. Jerome

Church Doctor in the West, Jerome (347-420), was born into a Christian family. He read Greek and Latin literature extensively, and treasured his library of pagan classics. Jerome was conflicted over how to reconcile the Bible's teachings with the pagan writers he admired. His dilemma was resolved by a dream:

Jerome was caught up in the Spirit and hauled before the judgment seat. Radiant beings asked him who he was. When he replied that he was a Christian, the judge told him that he was lying because he was a follower of Cicero, not Christ.

They ordered him to be scourged. He pleaded with the Lord for mercy, and bystanders prayed that the judge would give Jerome a chance to repent. After he took an oath never to read any worldly works, he was dismissed.

When Jerome awoke, his eyes were drenched in tears, and his shoulders were black and blue. From then on, he read only the books of God with great zeal.[112]

26

Dream Sharing Groups

Synesius of Cyrene laid out sound reasoning for discussing dreams and detailed the blessings we gain from studying our dreams.[113]

When we share our dreams in an atmosphere of prayer, trusting the Holy Spirit to lead us, there seems to be an intuitive sense operating. Since dreams contain universal truths, people around us often can recognize the metaphorical meaning of our dream symbols better than we can. This may help us find new meanings and perspectives we've overlooked.

My interest in dream groups grew out of my efforts to help others understand their dreams. I realized the need for support when learning the art of Christian dream work. I also saw the importance of sharing dreams and receiving feedback within the context of a Christian community.

Emphasizing the value of working with dreams in the larger community, Savary, Berne & Williams suggest, "We journey, not as individuals, but as part of an interrelated network of other individual journeyers."[114]

A dream sharing group offers a place to receive support, gather intuitive feedback, and benefit from the imaginative input of others. We also gain from hearing other people's dreams and the understanding they find in them. Watching faces light up when the Spirit of God witnesses to the meaning of a dream brings life to all of us.

Note: I do not advocate making major life decisions based on a dream, without confirmation from two or three other people.

1. Dream group technique: "If it were my dream ... "

To combat professional arrogance (the idea that only experts can interpret dreams) psychoanalyst Montague Ullman and others developed a dream group technique known as "If it were my dream ... ."[115] Using this approach, ordinary people can benefit from sharing their dreams, without analysis or interpretation by professionals.

Listening to what others suggest our dream might mean to them takes the pressure off us. They won't be trying to force their understanding on us. We can relax and be free to absorb whatever they say that rings true for us. It's a gentle way to keep the group safe for everyone.

This technique also allows us to distance ourselves from our own dream so we can listen for the inner *"Aha!"* the response of our spirit as they share. I have found this technique to be valuable in my dream sharing groups.

Here's how it works:

- Dreamer describes his or her dream as completely as possible.
- Group members ask for clarification of only the content and feelings related to dream.
- Members share their *feelings* about the dream—as if it were their own dream. To begin, members preface their remarks by saying, "If it were my dream, I might be feeling this ... "
- Members then work on the dream images as if they were their own, as if they were metaphorical expressions of something about their own lives, not the dreamer's. Always begin with, "If it were my dream, it might mean ... ," to acknowledge their ideas are merely *suggestions*.
- Dreamer responds to the suggested metaphors and feelings of the group, knowing that he or she has the final authority on the dream's meaning.
- Dreamers are free to say "stop," when they want to go no further in examining their dream with the group.

2. Leaderless dream group

A leaderless dream group, consisting of three to four people meeting two hours weekly, can work quite well for some people. First, one person tells a dream. In turn, the other group members comment on the dream *as if it were their own,* suggesting what it means to them. This process is repeated for the other group members.

3. Dream sharing guidelines

Sharing dreams may cause us to feel vulnerable, exposed, or ashamed. Following are some guidelines to help everyone feel safe:

- Always maintain a sense of sacredness. Keep in mind: dream work isn't about fortune-telling or playing with a new gimmick, but a way to receive divine counsel, instruction, guidance.
- Tell dreams in the present tense, as if the dream is being dreamed in the present.
- The dream belongs to you, the dreamer, *not* the group.
- Dreams can go into places where you are not ready to go, let alone talk about with others. You have the right to decide how deep you want to go with a certain dream. You may choose to use a hand signal that means *stop, no more; this is all I can accept right now.*

4. Listening tips

- When others share their dreams, listen in a caring way—don't judge, evaluate, or try to interpret it.
- Don't interrupt the dreamer. Avoid making comments or asking questions until they've finished.
- Always ask dreamer if they are open to receiving feedback.
- Be sensitive when you offer feedback to others.
- Never say with absolute authority, "This is what your dream means." Always suggest in a tentative way, "Do you think it might mean this?"
- Always respect dreamer's right to decide the meaning of their dream. The dreamer is the only one who can say with any authority what the dream means.
- Respect right of dreamer to decide how deep they want to go with a certain dream.
- You are present to help others experience more fully their dreams, rather than interpret them.

About confidentiality

Jeremy Taylor suggests the following thoughts about confidentiality: [116]

1. Members should agree at the outset to maintain anonymity in all discussions of dreams.
2. In the absence of a specific request for confidentiality, in discussions outside the group, no dreamer should be identifiable by their stories.
3. Whenever any group member requests absolute confidentiality, everyone must agree to keep it.

✉ 20th c. dreamer—Prayer group member

Catherine Marshall (1914-1983) cites an amazing dream example from a prayer group. A woman suffering from exhaustion and insomnia shared a dream about a baby who needed milk.

When the prayer group heard her dream, two people gasped—each of them had independently received the word that the woman herself needed milk.

Also, one group member reported receiving Numbers 12:1-10 that very morning—a passage saying the Lord speaks in dreams. When the exhausted woman consulted a nutritionist, she learned that she suffered from a serious calcium deficiency that's easily treated by milk.[117]

Part Five

Symbolic Techniques

Symbolic dream work refers to unlocking the meaning of symbolic material in our dreams and connecting with God's divine purpose in it. By interacting with its symbolic imagery, we enter into a kind of dialogue with God that allows the images to spring spontaneously alive with meaning for our lives. As our heart is touched, an *"Aha!"* may bring a sudden quickening, a *knowing*, that releases an overflowing emotion, welling up in our eyes as tears.

The goal is to find out what the symbolic element means to you in your own inner world and then connect its meaning to your life. This is the heart of symbolic dream work: unlocking the meaning of a symbol in your dream. In Part Five, I explain five steps you can use in symbolic dream work:

1. Identify the elements.
2. Amplify the elements.
3. Make personal associations to the elements.
4. Connect the symbolic meaning of the elements to your inner life.
5. Summarize what the dream might be saying to you.

I also describe some symbolic figures you will meet in your dreams, present principles to use in testing your interpretation, and lastly, highlight the importance of responding to your dream.

Dream work principles
☆ Identify every element; nothing is insignificant in the dream.
☆ To amplify an element, identify its characteristics and functions.

☆ When working with a dream, go where the energy takes you, to the association that brings up a surge of energy.

☆ Use questions to connect the symbolic meaning of an element to what's going on inside you.

☆ Write a short statement of what you think God is saying to you in your dream.

☆ The Holy Spirit must be the final witness to the interpretation of your dream.

☆ A fundamental principle of Christian dream work is that we must take action in response to a dream.

27

Identify Dream Elements

Early Church Father John Chrysostom said that the dreamer is not responsible for acts committed in dreams and should not feel guilty or disgraced by what he saw or did while dreaming.[118]

As you begin to work with symbolic material, the first step is to review your dream and note all of its distinguishable elements. This gives you a clear understanding of the exact details of your dream. Be sure to note every element you can recall, not only the visual, but other sense impressions as well.

Use the following list to familiarize yourself with the types of elements that might show up in your dreams. Remember, most of the symbolic images will come out of your own life, not someone else's. Also keep in mind what John Chrysostom taught: Don't feel embarrassed by any of your dream elements or actions (good to remember when you run around naked in your dream).

1. Identify every element of the dream

a) Setting—refers to the dream context or stage upon which a particular concern will unfold: location, landscape, scenery, season, time of day, weather, environment, inside a building. The most common dream setting is a building, typically a domestic place, such as a living room, kitchen, or bedroom.[119] (See #14 *Dream Stories* for more information about the setting.)

b) Buildings—note the description, condition, shape, type: rooms, floors, elevators, stairs, colors, age, location of any buildings. If the house is known, it may be calling attention to what you experienced or learned in it, or your relationships with people in it at that time. Unknown houses usually represent your inner self. Large public buildings, such as churches or hospitals, typically represent the functions they are used for. Churches may refer to your relationship to organized religion, to God, to your religious beliefs, or to your inner sanctum.

c) Figures, characters, people—take note of how many, appearance, gender, age, posture, hair, clothing. Note if they are known or unknown to you. Identify if any of them are family members, helper figures, celebrities, casual acquaintances, uniformed person, or composite figure. Observe if anyone is a nurse, engineer, programmer, salesperson, teacher, advisor, pastor/priest, monk, office worker, doctor, lawyer, police officer. Typically there are three characters in a dream, and strangers show up more often than family or friends.[120]

d) Wildlife—be aware of any animals, birds, fish, reptiles: number, description, condition, etc. Note any composite animals, ones that changed to another animal during the dream, or any talking wildlife.

e) Vegetation—identify any plants, flowers, vines, bushes, trees: description, condition, color. Notice if there is anything unusual about them.

f) Objects—note any suitcases, clocks, vases, crosses, computers, etc. Jot down any description, number, condition, color. Observe if there is anything unusual about an object, and whether it's familiar.

g) Vehicles & transportation or transportation hubs—identify any cars, buses, trucks, trains, railway stations, airplanes, airports, boats, docks, motorcycles, or ships. Note things like their age, condition, color, etc. Also observe who is driving the vehicle, whose vehicle it is (your mother's?), and whether you are in the backseat or in the driver's seat.

h) Action/activity—observe what the people or figures are doing, like searching, running, escaping, flying, traveling, eating, preparing, diving, swimming, boating, driving. If there is a series of actions, identify them all. More often someone will be running or walking. Other frequent activities are talking, sitting, socializing, or playing.[121]

i) Movement—be aware of such things as blowing wind, rushing water, swirling clouds, approaching storm, lightning bolts.

j) Emotions—recognize the different emotions or feelings in your dream to help you understand your dream's message (see #16 *Emotional Feeling*).

k) Physical sensations—distinguish any smell, sound, taste, physical pain, fatigue, exhaustion, ease, cold, hunger.

l) Spoken or unspoken words—record any dialogue, thoughts, statements, impressions, phrases, or conversations, spoken or unspoken, in the dream. Note who says or thinks the words or expresses the thoughts.

2. Include small details

Don't miss any of the details. I have found that even the tiniest, seemingly least significant detail can offer clues about the dream's meaning or the area of my life the dream is about.

Nothing is insignificant. Weather, time of day, lighting, condition of buildings, colors, hair styles, eyes—it's all helpful. As in mystery novels, little hints are embedded in the dream that can lead us to its meaning. Some clues suggest when or where the issue that surfaces in the dream first occurred in our lives.

🖹 21st c. dreamer—Jack Nicklaus

Renowned golfer, Jack Nicklaus, was unable to determine the source of a prolonged slump in 1964. Then he dreamed: He was hitting the ball quite well, and noticed that he was holding the club differently than usual.

Later, on the golf course he tried swinging the way he had done it in his dream, and it worked for him. His scores improved immediately, and thereafter he continued using the same technique. He explained that the idea for the turnaround in his performance came to him in a dream.[122]

28

Amplify Dream Elements

Church Father Synesius of Cyrene warns against using dream books to help understand the dreams of a given person, because each one has such a diversity of imaginative spirit.[123]

You've identified all of the distinguishable elements in your dream. Now you're ready for step two: amplify your dream elements. Amplification refers to describing an element and clarifying its objective connotation (what you already know about it). The goal is to shed light on the dream and create a larger warehouse of information for more insight or an "*Aha!*" to emerge. *Amplification is a logical activity, where you identify the typical characteristics and functions of each dream element.*

It's not difficult, so don't panic. Just choose a dream or a dream element that you feel curious about. You might want to choose the more highly charged image, the one that brings up a surge of energy in you.

The following questions will help you amplify the image in its inherent qualities and functions, before you color its meaning and character by making personal associations.[124]

1. Select the symbolic element you want to amplify

- Reread your dream record.
- Review the list of elements identified in your dream.
- Choose which element to amplify.

2. Note its chief characteristics

- Describe its main characteristics.
- What or who does it look like?
- How does it differ from others?
- How would you explain it to someone who has never seen it?

3. Identify its primary function
- Why does it exist?
- How is it used?
- What purpose does it serve?
- How does it differ from others like it?

⌨ *21ˢᵗ c. dreamer—Ralph Nault*

Recently, our friend, Pauline Nault, had an operation to have a cancerous growth removed from her breast. The night before the operation her husband, Ralph, had the same dream three times.

In each dream, a large angel was sent to Pauline and Ralph to watch over them. The message that came with it was, "I never forget my faithful servants."

29

Make Personal Associations

This figure of speech Jesus spoke to them, but they did not understand what those things were which He had been saying to them. – John 10:6

All the elements of your dream have been identified, and you've described their primary characteristics and functions. Now you can begin the third step: work with each element symbolically by making personal associations to it.

Select a symbolic element that holds a lot of energy for you, lift it out of the dream, and ask, *what does this image mean to me in my inner world?* Although your unconscious already knows what it means, you must bring it to consciousness so you can benefit from the energy it contains. This answers the questions: What does this remind you of? What comes to mind when you think of it? Your associations are key to unraveling the meaning of a dream.

When working with a dream, go where the energy takes you, to the association that brings up a surge of energy.[125] Making associations will help you clarify what this element means to you in your unique inner world and connect it to the dynamics operating within your soul. This is art, not science—stay in your right brain.

The art of "making personal associations"[126]

Remember what it's like to look through a stack of old pictures or your old school yearbook? As your mind drifts through past experiences, memories and feelings keep coming to your awareness. This is similar to what we do in making associations to a dream element.

We allow the subjective part of our mind to take us freely to other associations as we think of them. Spontaneous thoughts, feelings, sensations, intuitions, and memories simply bubble up into our awareness as we reflect on, or relate to, the dream element.

All you need is a willingness to let yourself go. As you ponder your dream, write out every personal association—word, idea, mental picture, feeling, or memory—that pops into mind. Note how intense your emotional response is to each symbol. This is key!

When you finish with one element, go back and repeat the process for some of the other elements if you like.

1. Make your personal associations

- Choose a dream element you want to work with symbolically.
- What does this element remind you of?
- What does it bring to mind: what ideas, pictures, memories, thoughts spontaneously spring up?
- What feelings pop up when you think about this element?
- How intense is your emotional response to it?
- What does this element mean to you in your inner world?

2. Role play the symbol

To help you make associations to each symbol, you might like to try role playing. Essentially you act the part of each dream element, speak on its behalf, or hold an inner dialogue with it. Or perhaps someone can ask you questions about it, enabling you to discover more information about it. You answer, of course, from the perspective of the *dream*, not your waking life. After you finish the questioning, assess how your answers relate to your daily life.

- Tell your dream in present tense, describing all the details.
- Role play each part, imagining each image (element) is a part of yourself.
- Speak on its behalf.
- What does it feel like to be this part?
- What does it mean to be in this part?
- Hold a two-way conversation with it.

3. Continue making associations until the "Aha!"

Continue to make associations until you experience an "*Aha!*" or an inner resonance. Because symbols are linked to energy deep within us, we may feel sparks fly when the connection is made. It may feel like a tiny click or subtle shift, often releasing a flow of life and energy inside us. (Remember, we talked about this in #6 *The "Aha!" Moment*.)

You may experience a sudden tearing up in your eyes when the "*Aha!*" occurs. When you sense this intuitive witness, you've stumbled into the symbolic meaning of the symbol—you have illuminated the "dark saying" (see #12 *The Language of Dreams*).

Making personal associations is not about interpreting or analyzing a dream symbol; it's about discovering what the image means to you in your inner world. Most dream images come from your own life experiences, and you chose them unconsciously because they are capable of connecting you to the unseen parts of yourself. Remember, *you cannot rely on any fixed meaning of your symbols.*

✉ 21st c. dreamer—Jane Doe

Recently, a woman e-mailed us a dream. She was asking God to show her how and where she needed to be healed in her soul when she received this powerful symbolic dream:

I am inside the atrium of my heart. Looking around, I see how beautiful it is. A glass door is at the front of the atrium. My husband and someone else are standing outside the glass door, because the door is locked. They call to me, "Unlock the door." I answer, "You can't come in here, because the dog will bite you."

The dog in her dream was one she recently owned, but she had to give it away because of its unpredictable aggression and biting.

30

Connect Symbolic Elements to Inner Life

Dreams are like roots that reach far down into the nourishing depths of the earth of our souls, and help energy flow upward so our growth and development are possible. – Rev. John Sanford[127]

We have mastered the first three steps of symbolic dream exploration: identify all the dream elements, distinguish their main function, and experience their power symbolically ("*Aha!*"). Now we're ready for step four: *consider how each dream element connects to what is going on inside us.*

Making Connections to Inner Life

Our goal is to relate the element to some behavior, personality trait, emotion, value, attitude, potentiality, strength, gift, or capacity within us. Making this connection helps to release the energy it contains, and enables us to bring it into our daily life.

Also we need to consider what to do with the information once we have gained it. How will we apply the insights to our daily life? What actions do we need to take? Learning to ask questions is a major part of working with dreams symbolically.

1. Search for connections

- What goes on inside me that this dream speaks of?
- What truth is it conveying about me?
- What is the dream trying to get across about my inner life?
- What inner states of my mind, attitudes, habits might the symbolic element suggest?
- How am I like that element: person, object, animal?
- When do I unconsciously exhibit the same attitude or behavior as that element?
- Do I have the same gifts, talents, potentialities, possibilities as they do? What part of me is that?

135

2. How does that inner part of you express itself in your life?

- Where can I see that same trait in my personality? My choices?
- When do I behave like that? In what situations?
- Where have I seen this functioning in my life?
- What part of me has that capability, potential, quality?

Identifying Symbolic Dream Figures

Let's describe some symbolic figures we will encounter in dreams. Some of these figures represent the deeper parts of our inner self. People, animals, objects, situations, and relationships portray the dynamic processes within our own personality. These dream actors give visual form to our values, attitudes, feelings, and psychological complexes. We might view them as personifying aspects of our personality.

To benefit from these figures we work with them symbolically: amplify them, make personal associations to them, and then connect them to our inner life. Our goal is to make conscious their connection to the dynamic energies within us, so we can become more alive, more fully developed human beings.

Following are some of the common dream figures you will identify. Certainly you'll run into other players in your dreams, but this gets you started.

Persona figure—clothing or nakedness

Early in our journey toward wholeness, we will likely come upon persona figures in our dreams. Originating from the Greek word for mask, persona refers to the roles we play in daily life—the face we show that is presentable and acceptable to others.

Christianity demands authenticity, calling us to be genuine people whose aliveness can touch others. Jesus calls us to let our light shine in the world and not hide it. However, we often keep our light hidden behind defense mechanisms, religious faces, and false humility. We smile, say good words, act spiritual, but feel radically different. We wear a mask.

Everyone needs a persona, but it should accurately reflect who we really are on the inside. When it doesn't, God may use our dreams to help us see this. Persona dreams help us notice how we relate to the people and situations in the world around us. *The persona is often symbolized as clothing (or nakedness), or some other outward aspect of the dreamer.*

1. To explore persona figures in your dream:

- Identify clothing items: hat, jacket, skirt, slacks, shoes, stockings, bathrobe.
- What are its characteristics? What is its purpose or function?
- What does this item bring to mind?
- Is anyone naked, or nearly naked?
- What does this clothing item (or its absence) mean to you in your inner world?

Shadow figure—same sex figure

Another figure that shows up in our dreams is called the shadow figure. Appearing as a *person of the same sex as we are*, a shadow figure may be somebody we know in waking life, someone famous, or a person totally unknown to us. Its purpose is to reveal neglected parts of ourselves that we are unaware of, parts that we need to acknowledge and allow Christ to transform and integrate into ourselves.

Frequently the shadow represents the unconscious part of ourselves we have failed to live out, because it demands too much responsibility. Often we see these unknown aspects of ourselves as tendencies in other people (the psychological process of projection).

Usually the shadow presents itself as a negative or inferior personality characteristic. But the shadow can also be positive, revealing unrealized potential and capabilities. Amplifying and making personal associations to shadow figures can help you recognize your unknown attitudes, feelings, qualities, and abilities.

Opposite-gender figures

Opposite-gender figures appearing in dreams are more difficult to understand. They may personify very important parts of our total self, as God created us to be. However, they might just be symbolizing something else, like a job.[128] We don't have to fear these figures—they merely represent unfamiliar dynamic energies within us.

In some dreams, opposite-gender figures may personify masculine or feminine traits that we all carry. Typical masculine characteristics: logic, abstract thought, authority, determination, goal-oriented action. Classic feminine characteristics: creativity, receptivity, relationship, gentleness, nurture, unconditional love.

Opposite-gender figures are extremely valuable in our journey to whole-ness. Every woman has some (largely unconscious) masculine aspects she needs to make conscious. A masculine figure in a woman's dream may be calling for development of her more outer, goal-oriented self. Similarly, every man carries some (largely unconscious) feminine aspects that he needs to relate to. A feminine figure in a man's dream may be calling him to relate to his emotional life, or challenging his willingness to love and be loved.

If we ignore these powerful opposite-gender energies within us, we may project them into areas of our lives where they don't belong. A man may place his unconscious soul-image onto a woman, or onto his work, obsessing over them. Or a woman may fall for a man who gives her spe-cial attention, unaware that she's not relating properly to the unconscious masculine part of her soul.

2. To explore the shadow figures & opposite-gender figures, use questions like these:

- Are you currently in relationship with this person?
- What time period in your life might the person relate to? What were you involved in at that time?
- What is the person doing in your dream? What attitudes or behaviors are they displaying?
- What memories, experiences, situations, words, or ideas do they bring to mind?
- If the figure is unfamiliar, do they remind you of someone?
- Is the unknown person a helper figure, a wise figure, a Christ figure?
- What kind of work do they do? What roles do they play in life?
- What set of beliefs do they function from?
- What are their positive & negative characteristics, traits?
- Is the person a positive or negative figure for you?
- What does/did this person, character, figure mean to you in your inner world?
- What inner states of mind, attitudes, or habits might the per-son suggest?
- How are you like this person? Where can you find this in you?
- Do you unconsciously exhibit the same attitude or behavior they have?

- Do you have the same gifts, talents or possibilities as they do?
- Why are they appearing in your dream at this time?

If the person, either same-sex or opposite-gender figure, is an immediate family member, you may want to first view the dream as an objective dream (#13 *Two Approaches*). Consider whether this dream is about how you are relating to that person in waking life.

⊟ *20ᵗʰ c. dreamer—Jasper Johns*

Jasper Johns, called one of the founding fathers of pop art, had a dream that inspired him to paint the American flag in 1954.

This work was the first of a series that revolutionized art in America by lifting commonplace objects to the status of art.[129]

31

Summarize Meaning of Dream

An uninterpreted dream is like an unopened letter from God. – The Talmud

When you complete the first four steps of symbolic dream exploration, one additional step remains. It's important to *summarize* what you feel is the purpose of the dream, the meaning it has for you, by *writing a short statement of what you think God is saying to you in your dream.*

Symbols are not as easily manipulated by our rational mind as are words or concepts. However, after we experience a dream symbolically, we need some conceptual thinking—words and sentences—to make it conscious and release its energy into our daily lives.[130]

Avoid putting yourself under strain to find the meaning of a dream. Only when we lower our ego energy (humble ourselves) can we hear or sense what the Spirit of God is saying. Don't try to force an understanding: let the meaning come to you.

1. Consider the following before summarizing your dream

Review these factors and reflect on how they relate to your life:

- Consider dream within the *context* of your life, the circumstances of your current situation. (#4 *Identify Current Concerns*)
- What aspect of your life is this dream concerned with?
- What might its biblical purpose be? (#10 *Biblical Purposes*)
- What type of dream might this be? (#11 *How Important Is This Dream?*)
- Is it about your outer life or inner life? (#13 *Two Approaches*)
- What insights did you experience while making personal associations? (#29 *Make Personal Associations*)

2. Write a clear statement summarizing your dream

Write a clear statement of what you think God is saying to you in your dream. Make a succinct summary of the central idea that the dream is trying to convey to you: note whether it arouses any feelings in you.

Often the simplest, shortest interpretations are the best ones. Include any final insights you felt during this process.

- What is the overall meaning of the dream for your life?
- Summarize your considerations by writing them down—allow the insights to flow.
- Write a simple statement about your dream's message or meaning. Read it aloud.
- What gift or treasure is the dream bringing you from God?
- What is it advising you to do?

3 Consider the many levels of your dream

Symbolic dreams are often multidimensional, containing many layers of information at once. The meaning of dreams can be considered from five levels:[131]

1. What might it mean on a personal level? What is it showing about your attitudes?
2. Does it show something about your personal relationships?
3. What might it be saying about your spiritual life?
4. Does it have meaning as it relates to your community or tribe?
5. Is it showing you something about the world at large?

21st c. dreamer—Kevin Anderson

Psychologist, Dr. Kevin Anderson, reported the following dream after he plunged into depression: I dreamed about a plane crash. My wife and children watched from a distance as a plume of smoke appeared on the horizon. "Was Daddy on that plane?" one of the children asked. "Yes," my wife said as the dream ended.[132]

32

Test Your Interpretation

Joseph said to them, "Do not interpretations belong to God?" – Genesis 40:8

Unlocking the mystery of dreams requires that we learn to discern and test our interpretations properly using biblical principles and guidelines. Our understanding of a dream should answer these questions: What is the central, most important message this dream is trying to communicate to me? What is it advising me to do? What is the overall meaning of the dream for my life?

Most importantly, the interpretation of our dream should arouse energy and strong feelings in us. This might be a good way to test the validity of our interpretation—if there is no energy (the *"Aha!"*), perhaps it's not the correct understanding.

Rely on the Holy Spirit

Since the interpretation belongs to God, the Holy Spirit must be the final witness to the meaning of the dream. As with any other attempt to understand the spiritual realm, we must learn to discern what is from God and what is not.

Working with our dreams requires us to exercise our spiritual senses, just as we do with someone's teachings, prophecies, visions, and audible voices. If we fail to recognize the witness of the Holy Spirit, we can be misled with the wrong interpretation.

Interpretation should not appeal to your ego

Although dreams certainly encourage us on our journey, they are not aimed at stroking our ego, telling us what magnificent creatures we are. If the understanding of a dream appeals to the ego or resists being tested, it is suspect immediately. A correct interpretation produces good fruit and humility. Dreams are intended to help us develop and mature into the whole person God desires us to be.

Avoid these two pitfalls:

1. Don't project your wishes onto the dream.
2. Don't try to make your dream come to pass, or to make your desire happen.

1. Apply biblical guidelines

Faced with any supernatural phenomenon, we must examine it carefully according to the Scriptures—no interpretation is valid if it contradicts basic spiritual principles revealed in the Bible. Any reality shown to us personally in our dreams can never replace or supersede the written word of God. We are to test everything and hold fast to what is good (1 Thess 5:19-21).

The role of the Holy Spirit is to glorify Jesus Christ—to take what is His and declare it to us (John 16:12-14). *A fundamental criterion for the truth and value of a dream interpretation is its orientation to Christ himself.* If an interpretation advocates a plan of salvation other than the Gospel of Jesus Christ, or if it steers us away from our Lord, it definitely does not come from the Holy Spirit.

Test your interpretation *against these biblical principles:*
- Glorifies Jesus Christ as your only Lord.
- Doesn't take away from the completed work of Jesus Christ.
- Doesn't violate the nature of Christ.
- Nurtures your faith, hope, and love.
- Contains nothing contrary to faith or morals.
- Affirms "the law of the spirit of life in Christ Jesus."
- Helps you live more fully the truths of the gospel of Jesus Christ.
- Encourages, instructs, or enlightens you—without lifting up your ego.

2. Try this test for interpretation

To check if an interpretation is from God—not the dream itself, but your *understanding* of it—assess it using the following principles. Does the interpretation:

- Give you comfort, or torment?
- Bring you hope, or despair?
- Produce pride, or humility?

- Bring peace, or pressure and anxiety?
- Bring inner freedom, or lay a heavy burden on you?
- Answer your prayer?
- Minister life or death?
- Show you how to solve a problem?
- Accuse you?
- Reveal truth about yourself that you need to see?

3. Seek confirmation from intuitive friends

If your interpretation involves major life decisions, discuss your dream with spiritually-sensitive friends. If you think the dream is about future events in your nation, submit it to recognized Christian leaders for their viewpoint. The Scriptures say, "In abundance of counselors there is victory" (Prov 11:14).

⌨ 21st c. dreamer—Christopher Bessette

Filmmaker, Christopher Bessette, risked his career and personal safety to capture the evil of sex trafficking on video based on his dream, where he saw a man whom he identified as a "producer." Then he saw a yellow map of Cambodia with a clock on the bottom. "I thought in my dream that I can't tell the time, but God answered, 'Now is the time.'"

Soon after, in a divine "coincidence," a Christian couple agreed to help him produce the film. Months later, when Bessette shared his "yellow map" dream with them, they unfolded the map of Cambodia they'd purchased in Phnom Pehn—yellow. Bessette's film, *Trade of Innocents*, reveals the everyday reality of rescuing girls from the horrors of the sex trade.[133]

33

Respond to Dream

After interpreting the King's dreams, Daniel rejoiced, saying, "It is He who reveals the profound and hidden things; He knows what is in the darkness, and the light dwells with Him." – Daniel 2:22

It is a fundamental principle of Christian dream work that we *take action in response to a dream*. When people in the Bible awakened from a dream, they acted upon it—they understood the importance of responding to God. When Samuel heard a voice calling him in the night (an auditory vision), he was instructed by Eli to respond to the Lord: "Speak Lord, for Thy servant is listening" (1 Sam 3:9).

Divine energy came to us in the dream, but now we need to release this energy into specific actions in our waking life. Performing some type of religious ritual might be valuable here: repetition and dramatic enactment of words can impress us so deeply that it reaches our inner world. Taking some kind of symbolic action does something that affects our soul.

Many dream communications from God are conditional: they require our response. God is trying to get our attention in the dream. He's encouraging us to grow up in Christ, become mature, and find our destiny. By responding positively to our dream, we honor God and the message He brings us.

Give God the thanks

Christianity makes possible a living relationship with the Creator, our Heavenly Father. When He speaks, we should respond, acknowledging that we heard Him and we are grateful for this. As the meaning of a dream opens up to us, we need to recognize it was God who gave us the understanding. Like Daniel, we then rejoice in the Lord, giving Him the glory (Dan 2:22).

1. Write them on the tablet of your heart (Proverbs 7:3)

Israel (formerly called Jacob) remembered his son Joseph's dream for many years: "And his brothers were jealous of him, but his father kept the saying in mind" (Gen 37:1-11). Israel never lost touch with the dream, because he kept it alive in his heart and mind by remembering it, even though the dream belonged to his son. Here are some ways to hold the dream in your heart:

- Continue to meditate on the dream.
- Remember it before you go to bed—re-experience its energy.
- Reread the dream from time to time.
- Continue to hold it up before God in prayer.

2. Take action—actualize the dream

Dreams often challenge us to take some *action* that is important to our personal growth. Kelsey says we need to actualize the dream by taking the necessary action it calls for.[134] Jacob, after receiving his legendary ladder dream, acknowledged God who gave it to him. He then built an altar using his stone pillow and poured oil on it (Gen 28:11-16).

Robert Johnson suggests we affirm the dream message by doing something to move it from the abstract level into the here-and-now reality of daily life. Some physical action—lighting a candle or even walking around the block, if done intentionally—can help ground the meaning of the dream in our practical everyday experience.[135]

- Take specific action to acknowledge that you value your dream.
- Make a list of ways you might use to respond to your dreams.
- What will you do with the information gained from your dream?
- Explain to a friend why it is important to respond to a dream.
- Think about how you can actualize your dream by actively meditating on, and bringing God directly into, this part of yourself.

3. Live with the dream over time

Due to the symbolic power of a dream's images, its energy may persist for a long time. Also, the meaning of a dream may continue to unfold or deepen for many years. In my experience, some symbolic elements of a dream I have understood immediately, but didn't realize other aspects until years later.

If you can't interpret a dream, try just living with it for a while. Gifts your dreams bring are often weeks, months, even years, ahead of your conscious understanding. Some dreams won't be understood, and the dreamer must carry them for years without knowing their meaning.

✉ 19ᵗʰ c. dreamer—Rev. A. J. Gordon

Baptist pastor, Dr. A. J. Gordon* (1836–1895), says his ministry was transformed as a result of the following dream: He was in the pulpit just about to begin his sermon when a stranger entered and passed slowly up the left aisle of the church, looking for someone who would give him a seat.

Half way up the aisle, a man offered him a place which was quietly accepted. Gordon's eyes were riveted on this visitor. He wondered, "Who can that stranger be?" He determined to find out. After the sermon, the stranger slipped out with the crowd.

The pastor asked the man with whom he sat, "Can you tell me who that stranger was who sat in your pew this morning?" In the most matter of fact way he replied, "Why, do you not know that man? It was Jesus of Nazareth." Seeing the pastor's great consternation, the man assured him, "Oh, do not be troubled. He has been here today, and no doubt He will come again."[136]

* A compatriot of evangelist D. L. Moody, Gordon established a church in Boston that was considered to be one of the most spiritual and aggressive in America. (http://en.wikipedia.org/wiki/Adoniram_Judson_Gordon)

Part Six

Dream Work for Healthcare Professionals

This section is for people working across the wide arena of holistic health—counselors, psychologists, therapists, coaches, spiritual formation mentors, clergy, chaplains, pastoral counselors, volunteers in lay ministries, social workers, hospice nurses, oncology staff, addiction treatment professionals, mental health counselors—who care for the body, soul, or spirit of others and desire more tools to help them.

Dear King Nebuchadnezzar,

Hey, for starters, mind if I call you King Neb? Nebuchadnezzar seems so pretentious—hardly very fitting for the message I have for you. Listen, King Neb, it's about that pride thing I've been trying to get through to you about. Haughtiness is not a kingdom virtue. (Not happy about all the sacred vessel stuff you stole in the Jerusalem raid, either, but we'll deal with that a little later.)

For now I want to deliver a dream to you that admittedly will shake you up a bit. I know your memory is not so hot, and you may forget the dream as soon as you awaken (a lot of people do that, and I'm not pleased with it, but what can you do?). But my guy, Daniel, has a direct pipeline to me, so I'll give him the info when it's needed. The key thing you need to know is that change is coming in your kingdom, and it's not going to be pretty.

O king; this is what you saw: a statue, a great statue of extreme brightness, stood before you, terrible to see. The head of this statue was of fine gold, its chest and arms were of silver, its belly and thighs of bronze, its legs of iron, its feet part iron, part earthenware.

While you were gazing, a stone broke away, untouched by any hand, and struck the statue, struck its feet of iron and earthenware and shattered them. And then, iron and earthenware, bronze, silver, gold all broke into small pieces as fine as chaff on the threshing floor in summer. The wind blew them away, leaving not a trace behind. And the stone that had struck the statue grew into a great mountain, filling the whole earth (Dan 2:31-35).

Respectfully yours,

Yahweh

Dream Work for Healthcare Professionals

King Solomon said that "counsel in the heart of man is like deep water, but a man of understanding will draw it out." – Proverbs 20:5 (KJV)

Everyone dreams every night. These dreams offer a powerful resource to healthcare professionals, shedding light on troubling life issues people face, including psychospiritual conflicts. Dream work creates opportunities for inner healing, psychological growth, and spiritual growth.

As a professional on the front lines of holistic care, you often hear dreams, including troubling dreams and nightmares, from the people you serve. This book contains the practical tools you need to help your clients, patients, congregants, or consumers benefit from the wealth of wise counsel contained in their dreams.

Dream Work, A Powerful Tool

Throughout history, dreams have played an important role in how God communicates and infuses His love into people's lives. Since Freud's and Jung's pioneering work with dreams, the field of depth psychology is the only helping profession that embraced dream work as a therapeutic tool.

Rev. Dr. Terrence McGillicuddy, Anglican priest and Christian psychotherapist, worked for 22 years as a hospice Chaplain. He discovered that dream work had the power to move a person from "a place of darkness and fear to a new place of light and hope."[137]

McGillicuddy reports that dream work offers clients an opportunity to:

- Find inner healing, psychological transformation, and spiritual aliveness.
- Connect to that which is repressed, freeing the way for psychospiritual individuation.
- Engage in a depth process exploring what is below the surface.

- ◆ Work through existential and psychospiritual distresses to an authentic and profound religious experience.
- ◆ Connect with God, to a transfigurative experience of His presence and love and the reassurance they are connected to that which is eternal.

Empirical research supports dream work

The benefits of dream work are exciting. Clients frequently rate dream work sessions as higher in quality, insight, and working alliance than regular sessions.

In 2009, Douglas Thomas, PhD, LCSW, reviewed 25 years of empirical research concerning the therapeutic benefits of working with clients' dreams. He found *substantial empirical evidence that therapeutic work with dreams is clinically effective.*[138]

According to Dr. Thomas' findings, therapeutic dream work is effective in the following ways:

1. Helps create positive therapeutic alliance, making it easier to bypass client defenses and engage resistant clients in initial phase of treatment.
2. Facilitates therapeutic process and greater depth in sessions; reduces risk of early termination.
3. Promotes personal self-knowledge and insight, a reimbursable mental health service activity.
4. Fosters meaningful behavioral changes.
5. Empowers therapists to introduce difficult and sensitive topics.
6. Provides meaningful data on client's psychological progress.
7. Offers a source of existential meaning and comfort for people near death.
8. Promotes healing and resolution of loss, grief, and trauma.
9. Facilitates group cohesion when working with multiple clients.

Dreamworkers, Not Interpreters

This book is not about becoming a dream interpreter or analyst. It is about learning *how to help people relate* to their dreams and make connections to their purposes and meanings.

Using the term *dreamworkers* allows us to move away from the analytical idea of professionals telling others what their dreams mean, i.e., "to point out, explain, or teach dreamers the meaning of the behavior being manifested in their dreams."[139] Instead dream work refers to helping people draw out the inner meaning embedded in their dream narratives.

Dream work describes how to approach a dream, interact with its pictures, images and symbols, and make felt feeling connections with its purposes. The interpretation is the end result of the work.

The International Association for the Study of Dreams (IASD) describes dream work in the following way:

> Any effort to discover, speculate about, and explore levels of meaning and significance beyond the surface of literal appearance of any dream experience recalled from sleep ... Ethical dreamwork helps the dreamer work with his/her own dream images, feelings, and associations, and guides the dreamer to more fully experience, appreciate, and understand the dream.[140]

Flexibility of dream work

Dream work does not refer to any single philosophical or theoretical perspective. *Dreams can be understood without a theoretical orientation.* There is no single strategy or technique for a particular dream that conveys the richness of dream work.

Working with dreams can be used in widely diverse settings, including individual and group therapy; pastoral, marital, and career counseling; medical facilities, nursing homes, clinics, hospices; recovery groups, community mental health; dream sharing groups, churches and inner healing. Dream work offers help for people struggling with issues such as divorce, depression, anxiety, PTSD, psychosomatic symptoms, addictions, life-limiting illnesses, neuroses, decision-making, and aging.

Christian psychiatrist Len Sperry says that, in marital and family work, dreams can have a therapeutic effect because they provide access into both the unconscious and the religious realm. Bypassing the client's defense mechanisms, the dream can get to the heart of the person's problem quickly, making them aware of their inner conflicts and unlived emotions. A dream may even point toward a solution.[141]

Social workers sometimes advocate use of dreams in counseling. Catalano uses children's dreams in his clinical social work practice, noting that "dreams provide a wealth of useful material about the issues, feelings, and memories most important to the child."[142]

Dream research shows that dreams representing traumatic events convey how the dreamer feels relative to the trauma, including helplessness, terror, and grief. Hartmann asserts that a dream can help the dreamer integrate a traumatic event into consciousness.[143]

You can learn dream work

This book gives you the tools to facilitate dream work with the people you counsel, mentor, or minister to. Its concepts, principles, and techniques are drawn from a variety of philosophical, spiritual/faith, and theoretical perspectives. These views include psychodynamic, neo-Freudian psychoanalysis, Gestalt, existential-phenomenology, existential psychotherapy, dream group theory, contemporary, orthodox Judeo-Christian, and cognitive.

All of these viewpoints have the common goal of helping dreamers to acquire understanding, insight, and awareness, to recognize their destructive ways, and to gain new levels of consciousness. Your worldview will influence how you think of your role as a dreamworker: a midwife or coach, a consultant or collaborator, an aide or interviewer.

In this book you will learn fundamental skills and dream work principles, collect an arsenal of strategies and techniques, and build a working vocabulary of terminology. The techniques that you are drawn to will depend on your theoretical view of what it means to be a human being.

Guiding Principles

The following dream work principles have been collected from philosophers, theorists and researchers throughout the last century. Perhaps in the future the new brain studies will enrich our understanding of the world of dreams and offer us new ways to unlock their mysteries. Meanwhile, here are the principles that I rely on:

1. Dreams are meaningful, practical, personal.
2. All dreams are not equally important.
3. Most dreams are about the dreamer, their current concerns or psychospiritual issues.
4. Dreams convey messages important to the dreamer's heart and soul.
5. Repetitive themes are more important, offering keys to the dreamer's challenges.

6. Dreams reveal something the dreamer does not know, but they never condemn.

7. Dreams tell the truth, honestly expressing a dreamer's true feelings.

8. Most dreams communicate using symbolic imagery.

9. Recognize word plays and puns.

10. There is no fixed meaning for any symbol.

11. Pay attention to the smallest details; they have a purpose and provide clues.

12. Archetypal (transformational) dreams offer a major shift in consciousness.

13. It is key to note the intensity of a dream and the dreamer's reactions.

14. Dreams emotionally link past information to current concerns.

15. Dreams can discharge energy, often unresolved emotional energy related to the day's events or even earlier experiences.

16. Some dreams will not be understood for many years.

17. Symbolic dreams are often multidimensional, containing many layers of information at once.

Ethical Guidelines For Dreamworkers

1. The dream belongs to the dreamer, not the dreamworker.

2. Dreamers have the right to share or stop sharing a dream.

3. Dreamers are the decision-makers regarding their dreams' significance or meaning.

4. Dreamers must be forewarned that unexpected issues or emotions may arise during their dream work.

5. Never say, "Your dream means this … ." Always frame your suggestions in a tentative way, like, "Could it mean this?"

6. Never tell your dreamers that you dreamed about them.

7. Never accept dreams of sexual abuse as confirmation of prior history of abuse.

8. Dream work must be grounded in your professional assessment of the dreamer's personality and the factors in the past that are contributing to their current issues.

9. Consider dreamer's philosophical, religious, and moral convictions.
10. Ensure you do no harm through errors of omission or commission.

Foundational Skills

As dreamworkers, you will rely on sound basic helping skills, spiritual attunement, and the skillful use of questions. It will help if you have some basic knowledge in related fields like psychology, spiritual formation, religion/faith—or have someone you can consult with.[144]

Before helping someone with a dream, you will want to know something about the dreamer's background. Following are some foundational skills to help you as you begin incorporating dream work into your counseling, mentoring, or ministering service.

How to record dreams

Since dreams do not originate in our conscious mind, it is almost impossible to recall them unless they are captured in some way. The easiest way to do this is to immediately record the dream, describing its elements. This technique explains exactly how to record a dream and what to include in the dream record. (See #3 *Record Your Dream.*)

Know what most dreams are about

If you understand what most dreams are about, you will have more confidence in knowing what to listen for as your clients tell you their dream. Often dreamers want to think it's about the other people in their dream, not themselves. In a few cases, this may be true. But most dreams are concerned with the dreamer's personal life, relationships, social environment, vocation. The dreams are linked to their psychospiritual growth, healing, wholeness, and fulfillment. (See #8 *Most Dreams Are About You!*)

Understand different types and purposes of dreams

Understanding the different purposes and types of dreams will enable you to determine quickly the area of the dreamer's life the dream is about, or why this dream comes at this time. Then you can choose the best dream work techniques. (See #10 *Biblical Purposes;* #11 *How Important Is This Dream?*)

If a person dreams about being back in their childhood home, then you know it is a historic dream dealing with issues that began long ago.

The techniques you choose will help them connect to any traumatic experiences, unresolved issues with parents, or destructive attitudes and beliefs they learned at that time.

Dreams may try to help your clients in the following ways:

- Recognize their distorted thinking and destructive attitudes.
- Solve their current problems.
- Understand the roots of their intra-psychic challenges.
- Show them their strengths, weaknesses, or deceits.
- Liberate their creativity.
- Inspire and expand their vision.
- Make them aware of another dimension beyond their daily awareness.

Know how to work with symbolic language

Seldom is a dream message conveyed unambiguously in clear, straight-forward speech. Most of the time, the message of the dream is obscure, consisting chiefly of picturesque symbolic images of varying complexity and vividness.

Each person has their own dream language. The meaning of any place, person, object, or symbol differs from dreamer to dreamer, even from time to time in a particular dreamer's life. Hence it is vital to know how the language of symbolism works.

Most people want to take the dream literally or as predictive of the future. They will need your help to look at the inner symbolic meaning of their dream images. (See #12 *The Language of Dreams.*)

Recognize typical dream figures

Dreams are populated by dream figures that reflect parts of ourselves, both familiar and unfamiliar. Some of these figures symbolically represent the deeper parts of our inner self and are called archetypes. These power-ful figures are infused with more energy, and are capable of changing our clients' conscious awareness of themselves. It is vital that dreamworkers recognize these transformative figures and know how to help their clients relate to them. (See #30 *Connect Symbolic Elements to Inner Life.*)

Recognize the "Aha!"

This is especially important. We need to recognize the moment a person touches, or comes close to, the inner meaning of their dream. You will see the "*Aha!*" in their body language, their face, their eyes. For me it is a sacred moment, because it is the work of the Spirit of God.

This will do so much more for a person than you could ever do for them—to discover how present God is to them. There is nothing more important that you can give someone than to *help them realize the presence of God is with them in their dream world.* (See #6 *The "Aha!" Moment.*)

Dream sharing guidelines

If you are interested in dream groups, this technique offers guidelines for sharing dreams in a group setting. You will learn the technique, "If it were my dream." You also can use this procedure with one person by simply pretending that the dream is yours. (See #26 *Dream Sharing Groups.*)

Suggested Strategies And Techniques

I. Reading assignments for your dreamers

Here are three techniques that will help both you and your clients. You can ask them to read these techniques and begin to log their dreams if they are interested in incorporating dream work in their counseling, mentoring, or personal ministry sessions.

1. Writing dream reports

Everyone dreams every night, one to two hours. By the time a person reaches age sixty, they've experienced five solid years of dreaming. So encourage them to write down their dreams, record them in some way. Emphasize how important it is for them to log their immediate Reaction at the same time. (See #3 *Record Your Dream.*)

2. Noting current concerns

Since most dreams come in response to the heart's concerns, it is vital that dreamers note what their current concerns were a day or two before the dream. This is key in helping someone connect to the meaning of their dreams. It is much more difficult to help people understand their dreams months or years later. (See #4 *Identify Current Concerns.*)

3. Using the TTAQ Technique

You can start your dreamers with the simple TTAQ (Title, Theme, Affect, Question) technique. Evidence shows that if they do only this, they will receive help with their dream. It also prepares the way for you to help them work with their dream. (See #5 *The TTAQ Technique.*)

II. Getting started with dream work

1. Invite person to tell you their dream

Invite the person to tell or read their dream to you, perhaps in the present tense. It is often helpful to ask them to repeat the dream a second time, allowing their emotions to connect to it. Encourage the dreamer to have faith in what the source of the dream is trying to tell them. It is their dream; it came out of their unconscious or heart. (See #9 *Dream Sharing*.)

2. Listen to their dream

The dream has a divine origin. As you listen to your client's dreams, you'll begin to get a schema, an idea of what God is trying to show them. Don't interrupt them. Wait until they're finished before you ask them to clarify something.

Just use your listening skills, recognizing that dream sharing works better if you allow it a sacred space. As they share, ask God, "Lord, what are you trying to show them in this dream?" Listen to the thoughts that spontaneously flow into your mind. Perhaps you will receive a *charisma*, such as a word of knowledge, as you listen. (See #7 *Approach Dream work Prayerfully*.)

3. Sketch their dream

Often I like to draw a sketch of a dream as it is being told. Or sometimes I invite the dream teller to draw it on a whiteboard. This provides a helpful visual reference while engaging in dream work. A picture is worth a thousand words. (See #15 *Draw-A-Dream*.)

4. Approach the dream

You have basically two options for how to approach your client's dream: 1) consider how it relates to their waking life (objective approach); or 2) focus on what the dream may be trying to show them about their inner life (subjective approach).

Since the relationship to a person's outer life is more readily understood, it may be easier to begin by looking for parallels between the dream and their outer everyday life. How does it reflect their coping methods, now or in the past? What kind of life situation might they be in that would lead to creating this metaphorical drama? (See #13 *Two Approaches*.)

III. Processing techniques

Read the introduction to *Part Three: Dream Processing* before processing some aspect of the dream. These techniques will help you to identify the area of the dreamer's life that their dream is concerned with. After that it's easier to help them work symbolically with the various people, animals, buildings, objects, etc. in their dream.

1. Process the structure of the dream

Most dreams consist of four parts:

1. Opening scene (dream setting)
2. Plot development (dream theme, story line)
3. Culmination of plot (because factor?)
4. Conclusion (solution or result)

Using a series of questions, *we help the dreamer draw out the information already visible in the dream structure and then link it to their outer everyday life or their inner world.* This gives us a basis for further exploration of the dream. (See #14 *Dream Stories.*)

For instance, identifying a "because factor" may help you identify the source of an issue, perhaps even indicate a solution. If the dream lacks a conclusion or has an unsatisfying conclusion, you can use techniques in *#22 Imaginative Strategies,* and *#25 Nightmares and Recurrent Motifs* to help your dreamer go back into a dream and rewrite the conclusion or change one thing in it.

2. Process the dream emotion or feeling (affect)

Sometimes a dream doesn't make sense, simply because it's about the emotion that the story is linking up for the dreamer. God is interested in those emotions because it leads them to where the wounds are. You want to use that emotion, because it offers you a key in your work with the client.

Help your client tap into that emotion, identify it, put a name on it. Many people don't know how to do that, but that's your job. Then you can ask, "What is that emotion, and where are you feeling that in your life now?" (See #16 *Emotional Feeling.*)

3. Process the activity or action in dream

Similar to processing the dream emotion, you use a series of questions to help the dreamer identify the action or activity in their dream. Inquire whether someone is driving, going backward, climbing a stairwell, going to the toilet, taking a shower, looking for something, searching for someone, dying, cooking food, being pursued, etc.

Then help them consider how it might relate to some area in their outer life or inner world. You will also want to note if they are a passive observer or active participant in the dream narrative and explore how that relates to the way they are living their life. (See #17 *Dream Action.*)

4. What is the dream ego figure doing?

Observing the dream ego figure's attitudes, choices and behaviors offers an amazing window into the dreamer's life. What choices did they make in the dream? Are they satisfied with their choices? What do they wish they'd done differently? You can use it to help them connect their daytime choices with what's going on within their soul. Are they living in harmony with their inner truth? (See #18 *Dream Ego Figure.*)

IV. Non-interpretative strategies

These strategies offer dreamers a more imaginative, playful and creative way to interact with their dreams. Here are several you may want to use with your dreamers.

1. View dream *as if* it were a parable

It can be useful to consider a dream as if it were a parable, a short story designed to teach some truth. A parable is not a direct statement that the ego understands, but rather a story that conveys meaning indirectly by analogy. Ask a dreamer to view the dream by musing, "*It is as if …* " and see where it leads them. (See #21 *Meditative Strategies.*)

2. Imagine dream *as if* it belongs to another

To help a dreamer put a dream outside themselves more objectively, suggest they pretend their dream belongs to someone else, perhaps a friend or acquaintance. This approach can help free their imaginative capacities by relieving any pressure they feel to get the correct understanding of their dream. (See #22 *Imaginative Strategies.*)

3. Role playing

Invite the dreamer to role play some of the characters in their dream, even creating dialogue with other parts. By assuming the various parts of the dream are facets of themselves, the dreamer can take ownership of their issues and feel some aspects of their conflicts from a little emotional distance. (See #22 *Imaginative Strategies.*)

4. Re-enter a dream

Encourage a dreamer to use their imagination to re-enter a troubling dream and possibly receive something positive from it. By using their God-given imagination, they may be able to rewrite an unsatisfactory ending or perhaps work through a traumatic experience. This is a good opportunity to invite the Lord right into their dream with them. (See #22 *Imaginative Strategies.*)

5. Imagery Rehearsal Technique (IRT)

IRT is a cognitive dream work technique that doesn't require re-experiencing or re-entering a painful dream. You can encourage a dreamer to develop new imagery for a dream and then rehearse the changed story. Based on the premise that reaction to a traumatic dream is a learned habit, the IRT can be useful for working with nightmares. (See #25 *Nightmares and Recurrent Motifs.*)

V. Symbolic techniques

Symbolic dream work involves knowing how to unlock the inner meaning of symbolic dream imagery. Here are five steps I often use: 1) Identify dream elements; 2) Amplify a dream element; 3) Make personal associations to an element; 4) Connect the dream element to their inner life; 5) Summarize the meaning of the dream.

The most important part of this process is helping your client make their own personal associations to an element and then connect it to their inner life. You will want to learn how this works.

1. Identify dream elements

Help a dreamer choose an element to work with by inviting them to select the one with the most attraction or intensity for them. (See #27 *Identify Dream Elements.*)

2. Amplify dream elements

Amplification means encouraging the dreamer to describe the chosen element, identifying its typical characteristics and functions. (See #28 *Amplify Dream Elements.*)

3. Make personal associations

Stay alert to the moment when they have an *"Aha!"* experience. *It's really important for the dreamer to experience the "Aha!" themselves.* (See #29 *Make Personal Associations.*)

4. Make connections to their inner life

Once the dreamer has experienced the dream symbolically, it is vital that you help them connect it to some emotion, behavior, attitude, value, etc. within themselves. *Once they make this connection, it helps release the element's energy and bring it into their daily life* (See #30 *Connect Symbolic Elements to Inner Life.*).

5. Summarize dream's meaning

As you are concluding the dreamwork, ask the dreamer to summarize in a simple sentence what they think the dream is trying to show them. (See #31 *Summarize Meaning of Dream.*)

Apply the new insights

As dreamworkers, we not only help the client unlock the mystery of a dream, but we can also help them engage in specific actions in response to the dream. We affirm the new awareness, the subtle change in consciousness, that resulted from their *"Aha!"* (See #33 *Respond to Dream.*)

Dream Work Is Not For Everyone

Here are some considerations to help you evaluate whether using dream work as a resource, tool, or therapeutic intervention is for you.[145]

1. Willingness to become comfortable working with dreams and encourage your clients/patients/congregants/consumers to tell you their dreams.
2. Readiness to open your heart to engage the dreamer's emotions and your own.
3. Openness to existential wisdom; respect for different ways of knowing.
4. Acknowledgement of a spiritual worldview.
5. Willingness to doubt your own analytical interpretations.
6. Capable of humility, recognizing that God grants the interpretation.

7. Recognize dreams speak out of a realm that is different from the ordinary world of reason and thought.
8. Capacity to engage in figurative and imaginative thinking, symbolic processing.
9. Acknowledge dreams as having contact with something more substantial than a person's mental thoughts or subconscious processes.
10. Recognize dreams can open a person to the realm of nature below conscious reality.
11. Willingness to assume the attitude of "not knowing" anything about the dream.
12. Recognize dreams can connect people more closely to the powers of the sacred; the people we serve might meet God, spiritual figures, or angels in their dreams.
13. Respect sacredness of dream telling.
14. Acknowledge your dependence upon the Holy Spirit.
15. Willingness to self-reflect, engaging your own psychospiritual processes, and examining your projections, transferences or countertransferences.

Whatever area of healthcare you have been entrusted with, you'll find that dreams are useful for helping people discover what God is saying to them about their issues and challenges.

Judith A. Doctor, MSW, RN

Appendix A

Dreams and Visions in the Bible

A study of both the Old and New Testaments shows that approximately one-third of the Bible involves dreams, visions, and other spiritual phenomena. Herman Riffel said that his review of *Strong's Concordance* yielded 224 direct references to dreams and visions, with approximately 50 dreams specifically mentioned.[146]

As you explore this rich scriptural tradition, ask yourself, What treasure did these people receive from their dreams or visions?

Dreams & visionary experiences recorded in the Old Testament

1. God established His covenant with Abraham in a dream/vision, assuring him of a great future (Gen 15:1-21).
2. Jacob received wisdom in his relationship with Laban in a dream, telling him what to do with the flock (Gen 31:10-29).
3. A dream warned Laban to be careful how he spoke to Jacob (Gen 31:24).
4. Joseph received dreams from God about his destiny. He dreamed of his sheaf standing erect while his brothers' sheaves bowed to his. In a second dream, the sun, moon, and stars bowed down to him (Gen 37:1-11).
5. Joseph's father, Israel (Jacob), kept Joseph's dreams in his mind for many years (Gen 37:1-11).
6. Pharaoh's butler and baker in prison experienced dreams revealing their immediate future (Gen 40:1-23).
7. When Joseph's brothers came to buy grain, God reminded him of his dreams about them (Gen 42:9).
8. Balaam's donkey saw an angel of the Lord standing before him in a vision. God also opened Balaam's spiritual eyes to see the angel of the Lord (Num 22:20-31).

9. Angel of the Lord spoke to Gideon at the wine press, giving him a vision and purpose for his life (Judg 6:11).

10. Midianite soldier dreamed of a bread loaf tumbling into camp, and as Gideon eavesdropped, another soldier's interpretation revealed God's protection over Israel (Judg 7:13-15).

11. Samuel's prophetic call came through a vision (1 Sam 3:4-15).

12. Nathan the prophet received the word of the Lord for King David via a vision in the night (2 Sam 4:4-17).

13. In Gibeon the Lord appeared to Solomon in a dream at night. God said, "Ask what you wish me to give you" (1 Kgs 3:5).

14. Isaiah received visions from the Lord containing prophetic warnings, encouragement, correction, promises, and the coming kingdom of God (Isa 1:1; 2:1; 6:1; 13:1; 21:2).

15. Jeremiah received visions, dreams, and prophecies (Jer 1:11-19).

16. Ezechiel the exiled priest/prophet saw a vision of a great fiery storm and sparkling wheels (Ezek 1:1).

17. God gave Daniel the ability to understand visions and dreams (Dan 1:17).

18. King Nebuchadnezzar received dreams and visions to reveal the future and the thoughts of his heart. When the king forgot a dream, Daniel immediately sought divine help to recall and interpret it (Dan 2:1-46).

19. Daniel correctly interpreted the king's dream about a tree in the middle of the world that was cut down (Dan 4:5-27).

20. Daniel had several great dreams and visions of his own (Dan 7:1-28; 8:1-27; 10:1-19; 12:5-6).

21. Amos, the Tekoan sheepherder/prophet, wrote about his visions concerning Israel (Amos 1:1).

22. Prophet Obadiah records his visions of what God said concerning Edom (Obad 1:1).

23. Nahum the prophet describes his vision called the oracle of Ninevah (Nah 1:1).

24. Habakkuk the prophet was directed by the Lord to record his vision, specifically to inscribe it on tablets (Hab 2:2).

Dreams & visionary experiences recorded in the New Testament

1. Joseph dreamed of an angel telling him to not be afraid to take Mary as his wife, even though she was with child (Matt 1:20).

2. God protected the Christ Child by warning the Magi in a dream, telling them not to return to Herod (Matt 2:12).

3. Angel appeared to Joseph in a dream, telling him to flee to Egypt and stay there, awaiting further instruction (Matt 2:13).

4. Once again an angel appeared to Joseph in a dream, telling him to go back to Israel (Matt 2:19,20).

5. Joseph received another dream warning him of danger, and he diverted his family to Nazareth (Matt 2:22,23).

6. Jesus referred to the Mt. of Transfiguration experience with His disciples as a vision (Matt 17:9).

7. Heathen wife of Pilate received a dream that warned him not to have anything to do with Jesus (Matt 27:19).

8. Zacharias encountered an angel in a vision, telling him God would answer their prayer (Luke 1:11-22).

9. Women at Jesus' tomb saw a vision of angels, telling them Jesus was alive (Luke 24:4,5,22-24).

10. As he was dying, Stephen saw a vision of the heavens open with Jesus standing at the right hand of God (Acts 7:55).

11. Saul encountered the Lord in an auditory vision, receiving revelations and direction (Acts 9:1-6).

12. God spoke to Ananias, a disciple of God, in a vision, telling him where to go, what to say, and what to do (Acts 9:10-18).

13. Angel of God came to Cornelius in a vision, informing him his prayers had been heard and telling him what he was to do—find Peter (Acts 10:1-8).

14. In a trance, Peter saw the sky open up and a great sheet lowered to the ground by four corners. The Spirit led him to Cornelius, who helped Peter understand the radical meaning of this iconoclastic vision (Acts 10:9-20; 11:5-10).

15. Peter said of his prison escape that he did not know whether what was being done by the angel was real, but thought he was seeing a vision (Acts 12:9).

16. In a "vision in the night" Paul saw a Macedonian man asking him to come to Macedonia and help. Taking action immediately, Paul changed his direction (Acts 16:9,10).

17. The Lord spoke to Paul one "night in a vision," telling him to not be afraid any longer, but to go on speaking and not be silent, because the Lord was with him (Acts 18:9,10).

18. Paul fell into a trance as he was praying, and saw Jesus telling him that his life was in danger. His testimony wouldn't be received, so he should leave Jerusalem and go to the Gentiles (Acts 22:17).

19. Paul, telling about his visions and revelations from the Lord, described being caught up into the third heaven (2 Cor 12:1-6).

20. John begins his famous Revelation book by describing his Patmos Island vision (Rev 1:9-20).

21. In a vision, John went through a door and entered heaven (Rev 4:1-3; 5:6; 6:8).

Appendix B

Scriptural Basis of Dreams

Nowhere in the Bible does it say that God will stop speaking through dreams after the New Testament era. There is no biblical basis for suggesting that God no longer uses dreams in our time! In fact, quite the opposite is true.

Christian use of dreams draws its authority from the following Scriptures:

1. Hear now My words: If there is a prophet among you, I, the Lord, shall make myself known to him in a vision. I shall speak with him in a dream. Not so with My servant Moses ... with him I speak mouth to mouth ... and not in dark sayings (Num 12:6-8).

2. Indeed God speaks once, or twice, yet no one notices it. In a dream, in a vision of the night, when sound sleep falls on men, while they slumber in their beds, then He opens the ears of men, and seals their instruction (Job 33:14-16).

3. I will bless the Lord who has counseled me; indeed, my heart [*inner man*] instructs me in the night [*while asleep*] (Ps 16:7).

4. There is a God in heaven who reveals mysteries ... He has made known to King Nebuchadnezzar what will take place in the latter days ... this was your dream and the visions in your mind while on the bed (Dan 2:28).

5. Behold, I will pour out My Spirit on you; I will make my words known to you (Prov 1:23).

6. I will pour out My Spirit on all mankind; and your sons and daughters will prophesy, your old men will dream dreams, your young men will see visions (Joel 2:28).

7. "It shall be in the last days," God says, "That I will pour forth of My Spirit upon all mankind; and your sons and your daughters shall prophesy, and your young men shall see visions, and your old men shall dream dreams" (Acts 2:16,17).

8. Things which eye has not seen and ear has not heard, and have not entered the heart of man, all that God has prepared for those who love him. For to us God revealed them through the Spirit … Now we have received, not the spirit of the world, but the Spirit who is from God, that we might know the things freely given to us by God (1 Cor 2:9,10, 12).

Spiritual principle: the mouth of two or three witnesses

The Christian use of dreams draws upon the spiritual principle, "Every matter is confirmed *by the mouth of two or three witnesses.*" First given to humanity in the Old Testament, this principle was confirmed by Jesus Christ in His ministry on earth, as recorded in the Gospels. In the New Covenant, St. Paul validated his ministry using this principle.

1. In the Old Testament Era, the Law of Moses established the principle that a matter could be established by the testimony of one or two witnesses:

A single witness shall not rise up against a man on account of any iniquity or any sin which he has committed; on the evidence of two or three witnesses a matter shall be confirmed (Deut 19:15).

2. Jesus corroborated this principle in the Gospel Era:

But if he does not listen to you, take one or two more with you, so that by the mouth of two or three witnesses every fact may be confirmed (Matt 18:16).

Even in your law it has been written that the testimony of two men is true [valid or admissible]. I am He who testifies about Myself, and the Father who sent Me testifies about Me (John 8:17–18).

3. The principle continues to be validated in the Apostolic Era:

This is the third time I am coming to you. In the mouth of two or three witnesses shall every word be established (2 Cor 13:1).'

In the same way God, desiring even more to show to the heirs of the promise the unchangeableness of His purpose, interposed with an oath, in order that by two unchangeable things, in which it is impossible for God to lie … (Heb 6:13-18).

Authority of the biblical witnesses

Listening to the voice of God in dreams and visions rests upon the authority of the following reliable biblical witnesses:

1. God Himself (Num 12:6–8)
2. Elihu to Job (Job 33:14–16)
3. King David (Ps 16:7)
4. King Saul (1 Sam 28:6,15)
5. Prophet Daniel (Dan 2:28)
6. King Solomon (Prov 1:23)
7. The Lord your God (Hos 12:10)
8. Prophet Joel (Joel 2:28)
9. Joseph (Matt 1 & 2)
10. Jesus Christ (Matt 17:9)
11. St. Peter (Acts 2:16,17)
12. Ananias (Acts 9:10–18)
13. St. Paul (Acts 16:9,10; Acts 18:9,10)

Author's Notes

Preface

1   Usually attributed to Rabbi Hisda, this thought comes from the *Babylonian Talmud, Tractate Berakoth, Folio 55a*, (translated into English by the Jews' College, London), quoted from the web site of *Come and Hear*, http://www.come-and-hear.com/berakoth/berakoth_55.html

2   Charles Fisher, "Psychoanalytic Implications of Recent Research on Sleep," *Journal of the American Psychoanalytic Association* 13 (April 1965), 20.

3   Douglas Thomas, "Dreams and Evidence Based Practice: The empirical case for restoring dreamwork to best therapeutic practices," retrieved from http://www.networktherapy.com/Douglas-Thomas/print.asp?pid=1530.

4   Herman Riffel, *Your Dreams: God's Neglected Gift* (Lincoln, VA: Chosen Books Publishing Company, 1981), 16.

5   Stuart A. Kallen, *Dreams, The Mystery Library* (Farmington Hills, MI: Lucent Books, 2004),10.

6   Judith Doctor, *Dream Treasure: Learning the Language of Heaven* (http://www.judithdoctor.com, 2011).

Introduction To Christian Dream Work

7   Riffel, *Your Dreams*, 23.

8   Morton Kelsey, *Dreams, A Way To Listen To God* (New York: Paulist Press, 1978), 100.

9   David Benner, *Care Of Souls: Revisioning Christian Nurture & Counsel* (Grand Rapids, MI: Baker Books, 1998), 170.

10   John A. Sanford, *The Kingdom Within: The Inner Meaning of Jesus' Sayings* (New York: HarperCollins Publishers, 1987).

11   Church Father Synesius, "On Dreams," *Articles on Ancient History*, http://www.livius.org/su-sz/synesius/synesius_dreams_01.html.

12   Scott Peck, *The Road Less Traveled: A New Psychology Of Love, Traditional Values And Spiritual Growth* (New York: Simon & Schuster, 1978), 243.

1 Take Dreams Seriously

13   John A. Sanford, *Dreams: God's Forgotten Language* (San Francisco: HarperCollins Publishers, 1968/1989), 102.

14   Kelsey, *Dreams, A Way*, 113-117.

15   Morton Kelsey, *Transcend: A Guide to The Perennial Spiritual Quest* (Rockport, MA: Element, Inc., 1981/1991), 65.

16   Morton Kelsey, *God, Dreams, And Revelation: A Christian Interpretation Of Dreams* (Minneapolis, MN: Augsburg Fortress, 1991), 166.

17   Synesius, "On Dreams."

2 God, Did You Speak To Me During The Night?

18 Kelsey, *God, Dreams, and Revelation*, 106.
19 John Sanford, *Dreams And Healing: A Succinct and Lively Interpretation of Dreams* (New York: Paulist Press, 1978), 12.
20 "A Canticle of Love," *Autobiography of St. Therese Of Lisieux*, http://www. ecatholic2000.com/therese/sos14.shtml

3 Record Your Dream

21 Kelsey, *God, Dreams, and Revelation*, 251.
22 Kelsey, *God, Dreams, and Revelation*, 100-101.
23 "Dreams and Visions Throughout Church History," *Communion With God Ministries*, http://www.cwgministries.org/dreams-and-visions-throughout-church-history
24 J.A. Wylie, "The Dream of Elector Frederick the Wise," *History of Protestantism* Vol I, http://www.lutheranpress.com/fredericks_dream.html.

4 Identify Current Concerns

25 Calvin Hall, *The Meaning of Dreams* (New York: McGraw-Hill Book Company, 1966).
26 St. Perpetua (c. 181–202). Her dream is recorded in *Martyrdom of Saint Perpetua & Felicitas*, http://www.christ.org.tw/patristics/nature_of_perpetua_dreams.htm
27 Doctor, *Dream Treasure*, 18-19.

5 The TTAQ Technique

28 Louis Savary, Patricia Berne and Strephon Williams, *Dreams And Spiritual Growth: A Judeo-Christian Way Of Dreamwork* (New York, NY: Paulist Press, 1984), 22.
29 Ibid., 23.
30 David Barton, "The Dream of Dr. Benjamin Rush & God's Hand in Reconciling John Adams and Thomas Jefferson," *WallBuilders*, http://www.wallbuilders.com/LIBissuesArticles.asp?id=10152

6 The "*Aha!*" Moment

31 Clement of Alexandria, "Chapter 9 - On Sleep," *The Instructor (Book II)*, http://www.sacred-texts.com/chr/ecf/002/index.htm
32 Catherine Marshall, *Something More: In Search of a Deeper Faith* (New York: McGraw-Hill Book Company,1974).

7 Approach Dream Work Prayerfully

33 Kelsey, *God, Dreams, and Revelation*, 104-105.
34 Ralph Nault, *Out Of Confusion: On To Spiritual Maturity*, http://www. ralphnault.com/books/, 150-152.

8 Most Dreams Are About You!

35 Savary, *Dreams and Spiritual Growth*, 39.
36 Synesius, "On Dreams."
37 From *The Catholic Encyclopedia*, http://www.newadvent.org/fathers/0310.htm.

38   Kelsey, *God, Dreams, and Revelation*, 133-134.
39   "A Biography of John Newton," *New Creation Teaching Ministry*, http://newcreationlibrary.net/books/pdf/285_JohnNewton.pdf
40   The dream is real and widely referenced; her response is from an unconfirmed source (A Rhode Island Newspaper).
41   Joe Nickell, quoted in Stuart Kallen, *Dreams, The Mystery Library* (Farmington Hills, MI: Lucent Books, 2004), 65.

9 Dream Sharing

42   Montague Ullman, *Working with Dreams* (London: Hutchinson and Company, 1979).
43   Clara Hill, quoted in Garry Cooper, "Clinician's Digest," *Psychotherapy Networker* 33, no. 5 (September/October 2009), 17.
44   This great war story from Judges 7:1-25 relates how Gideon followed God's specific guidance to victory against overwhelming military odds.
45   Doctor, *Dream Treasure*, 103.

10 Biblical Purposes

46   David Benner, *Care Of Souls: Revisioning Christian Nurture & Counsel* (Grand Rapids, MI: Baker Books, 1998), 165.
47   Kelsey, *God, Dreams, and Revelation*, 128.
48   Riffel, *Your Dreams*, 16.
49   S. Bradford, quoted in Van de Castle, 22.
50   Galen, *On the usefulness of the parts of the body* (Cornell University Press, 1968), quoted in Van de Castle, 65.
51   Jean Clift & Wallace Clift, *Symbols of Transformation in Dreams* (New York: Crossroad, 1986),117.
52   Len Sperry, *Spirituality In Clinical Practice: Incorporating the Spiritual Dimension in Psychotherapy and Counseling* (Philadelphia, PA: Brunner-Routledge, 2001).
53   "S. Basilii Magni, Commentarium in Isaiam Prophetam," quoted in Mark Virkler & Patti Virkler, *Communion with God* (Shippensburg, PA: Destiny Image Publishers, Inc., 1991), 63.
54   LaBarge, quoted in Van de Castle, *Our Dreaming Mind*, 440-441.

11 How Important Is This Dream?

55   Benner, *Care Of Souls*, 165.
56   Sanford, *Dreams And Healing*, 21.
57   Phyllis Koch-Sheras, Amy Lemley, & Peter Sheras, *The Dream Sourcebook & Journal: A guide to the theory and interpretation of dreams* (New York: Barnes & Noble Books, 2000), 85.
58   C.G. Jung, quoted in Mary Ann Mattoon, *Understanding Dreams* (Dallas, TX: Spring Publications, 1984), 140.
59   Jeremy Taylor, "The Dreamwork Tool Kit," http://www.jeremytaylor.com/dream_work/dream_work_toolkit/index.html
60   Eric Metaxas, "The Golden Fish: How God woke me up in a dream," *Christianity Today*, http://www.christianitytoday.com/ct/2013/june/golden-fish-eric-metaxas.html, posted 5/30/2013.

12 The Language of Dreams

61 Doctor, *Dream Treasure*, 190.
62 Paul Tillich, http://www.brainyquote.com/quotes/quotes/p/paultillic390301.html
63 "The Martyrdom of Polycarp," *Early Christian Writings*, http://www.earlychristianwritings.com/text/martyrdompolycarp-lake.html
64 Savary, *Dreams and Spiritual Growth*, 72.
65 Friedrich August Kekulé, "Famous Dreams," *dreaminterpretationdictionary.com*, http://www.dreaminterpretation-dictionary.com/famous-dreams-friedrich-von-stradonitz.html.

13 Two Approaches

66 T. White, quoted in Van de Castle, 22.
67 Joan Wester Anderson, *Woman's Day*, December 17, 1996, 156.
68 J. Lee Grady, "The coming tsunami in the Catholic Church," *Charisma Media*, http://www.charismamag.com/blogs/fire-in-my-bones/17042

14 Dream Stories

69 "Otto von Bismark's Dream," *International Institute for Dream Research*, http://www.dreamresearch.ca/interpretations.php?interID=156.

15 Draw-A-Dream

70 Doctor, *Dream Treasure*.
71 Koch-Sheras, *The Dream Sourcebook*, 223.
72 "Elias Howe," Wikipedia, http://en.wikipedia.org/wiki/Howe_sewing_machine.

16 Emotional Feeling

73 Karen Signell, *Wisdom Of The Heart, Working With Women's Dreams* (NY: Bantam Books, 1990), 16,17.
74 Riffel, *Your Dreams*.

17 Dream Action

75 "Constantine I," 2014. *Encyclopædia Britannica, Inc.* http://www.britannica.com/EBchecked/topic/133873/Constantine-I#ref384508

18 Dream Ego Figure

76 Herman Riffel, *Dreams: Wisdom Within* (Shippensburg, PA: Destiny Image, 1990).
77 Savary, *Dreams and Spiritual Growth*.
78 St. John Bosco, "The Dream of Nine," http://saintbosco.org/books/bosco05/

19 Dream Words

79 "Mont Saint Michel, the Wonder of the West," *Tradition in Action*, http://www.traditioninaction.org/History/A_025_Mont-1.htm

20 Dream Intensity

80 Robert Johnson, *Inner Work: Using Dreams & Imagination For Personal Growth* (New York: HarperCollins Publishers, 1986).
81 Kelsey, *Transcend*, 63.

82 *Sports Illustrated*, April 8, 1974, quoted in Van de Castle, 15.

Part Four Non-Interpretive Strategies

83 Benner, *Care Of Souls*, 160.

21 Meditative Strategies

84 Kelsey, *Dreams, A Way*, 101.

85 *Webster's New Universal Unabridged Dictionary* (2003).

86 Watchman Nee, *The Spiritual Man* (New York: Christian Fellowship Publishers, 1977).

87 Abraham Heschel, *God In Search Of Man: A Philosophy of Judaism* (New York: Farrar, Straus & Giroux, 1955), 148.

88 Terrence McGillicuddy, *Sacred Dreams & Life Limiting Illness: A Depth Psychospiritual Approach* (Bloomington, IN: WestBow Press, 2013), Kindle edition.

89 James Hillman, quoted in Sanford, *The Kingdom Within*, 57.

90 McGillicuddy, *Sacred Dreams*, 20.

91 Sanford, *Dreams And Healing*, 58.

92 Kelsey, *Dreams, A Way*, 101.

93 Benner, *Care Of Souls*, 170-171.

94 Mark Virkler & Patti Virkler, *Communion with God* (Shippensburg, PA: Destiny Image Publishers, Inc., 1991).

22 Imaginative Strategies

95 "The Teachings of Maimonides," *The Internet Archive*, http://www.archive.org/stream/teachingsofmaimo032353mbp/teachingsofmaimo032353mbp_djvu.txt

96 Johnson, *Inner Work*, 4.

97 The Saturday Evening Post web site, http://www.saturdayeveningpost.com/2010/03/20/archives/post-perspective/imagination-important-knowledge.html.

98 Janie Rhyne, quoted by Judith Rubin in *Approaches to Art Therapy: Theory and Technique*, 2nd ed. (Brunner-Routledge: New York, NY, 2001).

99 Savary, *Dreams and Spiritual Growth*.

100 David Mindell, "Automation's Finest Hour: Bell Labs and Automatic Control in World War II," *IEEE Control Systems Society*, December, 1995, 73, http://ieeecss.org/CSM/library/1995/dec1995/05-BellLabsnAutoCtrl.pdf

23 Dream Questions

101 Savary, *Dreams and Spiritual Growth*.

102 Robert Van de Castle, *Our Dreaming Mind* (New York: Ballantine Books, 1994), 25-26.

24 Dream Dialogue

103 Athanasius, "Against the Heathen," *Christian Classics Ethereal Library*, http://www.ccel.org/ccel/schaff/npnf204.txt (accessed June 1, 2013).

104 Benner, *Care Of Souls*, 181.

105 Savary, *Dreams and Spiritual Growth,* 60.

106 Van de Castle, *Our Dreaming Mind*, 81.

25 Nightmares and Recurrent Motifs

107 Jeremy Taylor, "The Dreamwork Tool Kit," http://www.jeremytaylor.com/dream_work/dream_work_toolkit/index.html.
108 "Dreaming takes the sting out of painful memories, research shows," *Annals of the American Psychotherapy Association*, 15:1 (Spring 2012), 9.
109 Ernest Hartmann, quoted in S. Ringel, "Dreaming and listening: a final journey," *Clinical Social Work Journal*, 30(4) (2002), 359-369.
110 Jeremy Taylor, "Recurring Dreams," Retrieved from http://www.jeremytaylor.com/dream_work/recurring_dreams/index.html.
111 Barry Krakow, quoted in Clara Hill and Sarah Knox, "The Use of Dreams in Modern Psychotherapy," *Marquette University ePublications*, http://epublications.marquette.edu/cgi/viewcontent.cgi?article=1130&context=edu_fac
112 Kelsey, *God, Dreams, and Revelation*, 136-137.

26 Dream Sharing Groups

113 Synesius, "On Dreams."
114 Savary, *Dreams and Spiritual Growth*, 175.
115 Montague Ullman, quoted in Koch-Sheras, *The Dream Sourcebook*, 68.
116 Jeremy Taylor, "The Dreamwork Tool Kit," Retrieved from http://www.jeremytaylor.com/pages/toolkit.html.
117 Marshall, *Something More*.

27 Identify Dream Elements

118 Kelsey, *God, Dreams, and Revelation*, 128.
119 Mark O'Connell, Raje Airey, Richard Craze, *The Illustrated Encyclopedia Of Symbols, Signs & Dream Interpretation* (Fall River Press, NY, 2009), 275.
120 Ibid., 275.
121 Ibid., 275.
122 John and Mariette Glanville, "Famous Dreams," *Dreaminterpretation-Dictionary.com*, 2011, http://www.dreaminterpretation-dictionary.com/famous-dreams-jack-nicklaus.html

28 Amplify Dream Elements

123 Synesius, "On Dreams."
124 Savary, *Dreams and Spiritual Growth*, 78.

29 Make Personal Associations

125 Johnson, *Inner Work*, 56.
126 Ibid., 52.

30 Connect Symbolic Elements To Inner Life

127 Sanford, *Dreams And Healing*, 11.
128 For a fuller discussion of this dream figure see Doctor, *Dream Treasure*, 211-215.
129 "Global Gallery," *Bentley Global Arts Group, LLC*, http://www.globalgallery.com/detail/89160/disco/johns-target

31 Summarize Meaning Of Dream

130 Savary, *Dreams and Spiritual Growth*, 73.

131 Ibid., 152.

132 Kevin Anderson, "Dark Passage: Suffering and the Quest for Wisdom," *Psychotherapy Networker*, retrieved from http://www.psychotherapynetworker.org/magazine/recentissues/2013-marapr/item/2094-dark-passage.

32 Test Your Interpretation

133 Anthony Petrucci, 2012. "Prophetic Dream Drives Sex Trade Film Production." *CharismaNews*, http://www.charismanews.com/culture/33526-prophetic-dream-drives-feature-length-film-production

33 Respond To Dream

134 Morton Kelsey, *Adventure Inward: Christian growth through personal journal writing* (Augsburg Publishing House: Minneapolis, MN, 1980), 119.

135 Johnson, *Inner Work*, 97-107.

136 "How Christ Came to Church," The Spiritual Biography of A.J. Gordon, http://www.leaderu.com/orgs/bpf/lguide/appendix03.html.

Part Six   Dream Work For Healthcare Professionals

137 McGillicuddy, *Sacred Dreams*.

138 Douglas Thomas, "Dreams and Evidence Based Practice: The empirical case for restoring dreamwork to best therapeutic practices," retrieved from http://www.networktherapy.com/Douglas-Thomas/print.asp?pid=1530.

139 "Ethics and Privacy", *International Association for the Study of Dreams*, retrieved from http://www.asdreams.org/ethics-and-privacy/.

140 Ibid.

141 Sperry, *Spirituality In Clinical Practice*.

142 Sackheim & Catalano, quoted in Urdang, Esther. *Human Behavior in the Social Environment: Interweaving the Inner and Outer Worlds* (New York, NY: The Haaworth Social Work Practice Press, 2002), 45.

143 Ernest Hartmann, "Outline for a theory on the nature and functions of dreaming," *Dreaming* 6(2) (1996). (Presented at the 13th International Conference of the Association for the Study of Dreams, Berkley, CA,1996).

144 Hartmann, "Outline for a theory."

145 Douglas Thomas, "An Invitation to Soulful Living: 3 Reasons to Work with Dreams," Dr. Douglas Thomas web site, http://drdouglasthomas.com/DT_images/WRITING_Dreaming_Essay.pdf

Appendix A   Dreams & Visions In The Bible

146 Riffel, *Your Dreams*.

Bibliography

Athanasius. "Against the Heathen." *Christian Classics Ethereal Library*, http://www.ccel.org/ccel/schaff/npnf204.txt

Barton, David, "*The Dream of Dr. Benjamin Rush & God's Hand in Reconciling John Adams and Thomas Jefferson.*" WallBuilders, http://www.wallbuilders.com/LIBissuesArticles.asp?id=10152

Benner, David. *Care Of Souls: Revisioning Christian Nurture & Counsel.* Grand Rapids, MI: Baker Books, 1998.

Blum, H. "The Writing and Interpretation of Dreams." *Psychoanalytic Psychology* 17(4) (2000).

Brisling, Scott and Mike Jones. *Understanding Dreams From God.* Pasadena, CA: William Carey Library, 2004.

Catholic Encyclopedia, http://www.newadvent.org/fathers/0310.htm

Cirlot, J.E. *A Dictionary Of Symbols* 2nd ed. New York: Philosophical Library, 1972.

Clement of Alexandria, Chapter 9 - On Sleep, *The Instructor (Book II)*, http://www.sacred-texts.com/chr/ecf/002/index.htm

Clift, Jean and Wallace Clift. *Symbols of Transformation in Dreams.* New York: Crossroad, 1986.

Crisp, Anthony. *Dream Dictionary: A Guide To Dreams And Sleep Experiences.* New York, NY: Dell Publishing, 1990.

Crisp, Tony. *Dream Dictionary: An A To Z Guide to Understanding Your Unconscious Mind.* New York: Dell Publishing, 2002.

Delaney, G (ed.). *New Directions in Dream Interpretation.* Albany, NY: State University of New York Press, 1993.

Delaney, G. *Living Your Dreams.* New York: HarperCollins, 1979.

Doctor, Judith. *Dream Treasure: Learning the Language of Heaven.* (http://www.judithdoctor.com, 2011).

Doctor, Judith. "*Resource Manual of Spiritual Interventions.*" (Unpublished, 2005).

Doctor, Judith. "Summary: Parallels Between Jungian and Black African Views on Dreams." (unpublished paper, 2003).

"Dreaming takes the sting out of painful memories research shows" (Nov. 23, 2011). *Annals of the American Psychotherapy Association.* Accessed from Expanded Academic ASAP - Document.mht

"Elias Howe," Wikipedia, http://en.wikipedia.org/wiki/Howe_sewing_machine

Encyclopedia Britannica, 2008, http://www.britannica.com/eb/topic-383152/Battle-of-Milvian-Bridge

"Ethics and Privacy," *International Association for the Study of Dreams*, http://www.asdreams.org/ethics-and-privacy/

Fisher, Charles. "Psychoanalytic Implications of Recent Research on Sleep." *Journal of the American Psychoanalytic Association 13* (April 1965): 20.

Gordon, A. J., http://www.lectionarysermons.com/ADV4-98.html (accessed May 31, 2013) .

Hartmann, Ernest. *Dreams and Nightmares: The Origin and Meaning of Dreams.* New York: Perseus Publishing, 1998.

Hartmann, Earnest. "Outline for a theory on the nature and functions of dreaming." *Dreaming* 6(2) (1996). (Presented at the 13th International Conference of the Association for the Study of Dreams, 1996).

Hartwell, George. *Dreams for Inner Healing.* http://www.healmylife.com/articles/inner%20healing/dreams%20for%20inner%20healing.html

Heschel, Abraham. *God In Search Of Man: A Philosophy of Judaism.* New York: Farrar, Straus & Giroux, 1955.

Hill, C.E., R.A. Diemer, & K.J. Heaton. "Dream interpretation sessions: Who volunteers, who benefits, and what volunteer clients view as most and least helpful." *Journal of Counseling Psychology,* 44(1) (1997): 53-62.

Hill, Clara, and Sarah Knox, "The Use of Dreams in Modern Psychotherapy." *Marquette University ePublications.* http://epublications.marquette.edu/cgi/viewcontent.cgi?article=1130&context=edu_fac

Hill, Clara, as cited in Garry Cooper, "Clinician's Digest." *Psychotherapy Networker* 33, no. 5 (September/October 2009): 17.

Hill, Clara. *Working with Dreams in Psychotherapy.* New York: The Guilford Press, 1996.

"How Christ Came to Church." *The Spiritual Biography of A.J. Gordon.* http://www.leaderu.com/orgs/bpf/lguide/appendix03.html

International Association for the Study of Dreams (IASD). (2001) "Ethical Criteria for Dreamwork Training." http://www.asdreams.org/index.htm

Bibliography

Johnson, Robert. *Inner Work: Using Dreams & Imagination For Personal Growth.* New York: HarperCollins Publishers, 1986.

Kallen, Stuart A. *Dreams, The Mystery Library.* Farmington Hills, MI: Lucent Books, 2004.

Kekulé, Friedrich August. "Famous Dreams." *dreaminterpretationdictionary. com,* http://www.dreaminterpretation-dictionary.com/famous-dreams-friedrich-von-stradonitz.html

Kelsey, Morton. *Adventure Inward: Christian Growth Through Personal Journal Writing.* Augsburg Publishing House: Minneapolis, MN, 1980.

Kelsey, Morton. *Dreams, A Way To Listen To God.* New York: Paulist Press, 1978.

Kelsey, Morton. *Dreams, The Dark Speech Of The Spirit: A Christian Interpretation.* New York: Doubleday & Co, 1968.

Kelsey, Morton. *God, Dreams, And Revelation: A Christian Interpretation Of Dreams.* Minneapolis, MN: Augsburg Fortress, 1991.

Kelsey, Morton. *The Other Side of Silence: A Guide to Christian Meditation.* New York: Paulist Press, 1976.

Kelsey, Morton. *Transcend: A Guide to The Perennial Spiritual Quest.* Rockport, MA: Element, Inc., 1981/1991.

Koch-Sheras, Phyllis & Amy Lemley & Peter Sheras. *The Dream Sourcebook.* Los Angeles: Lowell House, 1995.

Koch-Sheras, Phyllis & Amy Lemley & Peter Sheras. *The Dream Sourcebook & Journal: A Guide To The Theory And Interpretation Of Dreams.* New York: Barnes & Noble Books, 2000.

Krakow, B. & Joseph Neidhardt. *Conquering Bad Dreams & Nightmares: A Guide to Understand, Interpretation, and Cure.* New York: Berkley Books, 1992. Gives step-by-step instruction on working to diminish and eliminate nightmares and repetitive dreams.

Lasley, Justina. *Honoring the Dream: A Handbook for Dream Group Leaders.* New York: DreamsWork, 2004.

Martinez, R. "Dreams of Another Are All About the Dreamer." *Addiction Professional* 1 (2006): 42-43.

Martinez, R. "Introducing Dreamwork to the Group Setting." *Addiction Professional* 5 (2006): 55-56.

Martinez, R. "Some Resources to Assist In Dreamwork." *Addiction Professional* 9 (2006): 56-57.

Marshall, Catherine. *Something More: In Search of a Deeper Faith*. NY: McGraw-Hill Book Company, 1974.

Matthews, Boris, ed. *The Herder Symbol Dictionary of Symbols: Symbols from Art, Archeology, Mythology, Literature, and Religion*. New York: Continuum International Publishing Group, 1986/1993.

Mattoon, Mary Ann. *Understanding Dreams*. Dallas, TX: Spring Publications, 1984.

McGillicuddy, Terence. *Sacred Dreams & Life Limiting Illness: A Depth Psychospiritual Approach*. (Bloomington, IN: WestBow Press, 2013), Kindle edition.

Meier, P. & Robert Wise. *Windows Of The Soul: A Look At Dreams And Their Meanings*. Nashville, TN: Thomas Nelson Publishers, 1995.

Metaxas, Eric. "The Golden Fish: How God woke me up in a dream." *Christianity Today*. http://www.christianitytoday.com/ct/2013/june/golden-fish-eric-metaxas.html, posted 5/30/2013.

Mindell, David. "Automation's Finest Hour: Bell Labs and Automatic Control in World War II." *IEEE Control Systems Society*. December, 1995, 73. http://ieeecss.org/CSM/library/1995/dec1995/05-BellLabsnAutoCtrl.pdf

Nault, Ralph. *Led by the Spirit: Learn how to know what God is saying to you*. http://www.ralphnault.com/books/.

Nault, Ralph. *Out Of Confusion: On To Spiritual Maturity*. http://www.ralphnault.com/books/.

Nee, Watchman. *The Spiritual Man*. New York: Christian Fellowship Publishers, 1977.

O'Connell, Mark and Raje Airey & Richard Craze. *The Illustrated Encyclopedia Of Symbols, Signs & Dream Interpretation*. New York: Fall River Press, 2009.

Peck, Scott. *The Road Less Traveled: A New Psychology Of Love, Traditional Values And Spiritual Growth*. New York: Simon & Schuster, 1978, 243.

Riffel, Herman. *Dreams: Wisdom Within*. Shippensburg, PA: Destiny Image, 1990.

Riffel, Herman. *Your Dreams: God's Neglected Gift*. Lincoln, VA: Chosen Books Publishing Company, 1981.

Riffel, Herman. http://www.dreamsinfo.com

Ringel, Shoshana. "Dreaming and listening: a final journey." *Clinical Social Work Journal* 30(4) (Winter 2002): 349-359.

Rubin, Judith. *Approaches to Art Therapy: Theory and Technique,* 2ⁿᵈ ed. New York, NY: Brunner-Routledge, 2001.

Sackheim & Catalano. Quoted in Ester Urdang, *Human Behavior in the Social Environment: Interweaving the Inner and Outer Worlds.* New York, NY: The Haaworth Social Work Practice Press, 2002.

Sanford, John A. *Dreams: God's Forgotten Language.* San Francisco: HarperCollins Publishers, 1968/1989.

Sanford, John A. *Dreams And Healing: A Succinct and Lively Interpretation of Dreams.* New York: Paulist Press, 1978.

Sanford, John A. *Healing and Wholeness.* New York: Paulist Press, 1977.

Savary, Louis & Patricia Berne & Strephon Williams. *Dreams And Spiritual Growth: A Judeo-Christian Way Of Dreamwork.* New York, NY: Paulist Press, 1984.

Signell, Karen. *Wisdom Of The Heart, Working With Women's Dreams.* New York: Bantam Books, 1990.

Sperry, Len. *Spirituality In Clinical Practice: Incorporating the Spiritual Dimension in Psychotherapy and Counseling.* Philadelphia, PA: Brunner-Routledge, 2001.

Stone, Perry. *How to Interpret Dreams and Visions: Understanding God's Warnings and Guidance.* Lake Mary, FL: Charisma House Publishing, 2011.

Strong, J. *Strong's Exhaustive Concordance of the Bible.* Nashville, TN: Abingdon. 1894/1978.

Synesius, "On Dreams," *Articles on Ancient History.* http://www.livius.org/su-sz/synesius/synesius_dreams_01.html/

Taylor, Jeremy. *Dreamwork: Techniques for Discovering the Creative Power in Dreams.* New York, NY: Paulist Press, 1983.

Taylor, Jeremy (2005). http://www.jeremytaylor.com/pages/toolkit.html.

The Catholic Encyclopedia. See *Catholic Encyclopedia.*

Thomas, Douglas. "An Invitation to Soulful Living: 3 Reasons to Work with Dreams." Dr. Douglas Thomas web site, http://drdouglasthomas.com/Trainings.html/

Thomas, Douglas. "Dreams and Evidence Based Practice: The empirical case for restoring dreamwork to best therapeutic practices (2009)." *Psychotherapy Networker.* http://www.networktherapy.com/Douglas-Thomas/print.asp?pid=1530

Thomas, Douglas. http://drdouglasthomas.com/Trainings.html.

Ullman, Montague. *Appreciating Dreams: A Group Approach*. Thousand Oaks, CA: Sage Publications, 1996.

Ullman, Montague. "Dreams: An Under Appreciated Natural Resource" (1983). http://siivola.org/monte/papers_grouped/uncopyrighted/Dreams/Dreams_-_An_Under_Appreciated_Natural_Resource.htm

Ullman, Montague. (date unknown, after 1996) "The Significance of Dreams in a Dream Deprived Society." *New Directions in Dream Interpretation*. Ed. Gayle Delaney. http://siivola.org/monte/papers_grouped/uncopyrighted/Dreams/significance_of_dreams_in_a_dream_deprived_society.htm.

Ullman, Montague. *Working with Dreams*. London: Hutchinson and Company, 1979.

Van Breda, A.D. "Parallels between Jungian and black African views on dreams." *Clinical Social Work Journal*, 27(2) (1999): 141-155.

Van de Castle, Robert. http://www.ourdreamingmind.net/Consult.html.

Van de Castle, Robert. *Our Dreaming Mind*. New York, NY: Ballantine Books, 1994.

Van de Kemp, H. (2005) "Dreams and recovery from trauma." *Journal of Psychology and Theology* 33(4): 13-15.

Virkler, Mark & Patti Virkler. *Communion with God*. Shippensburg, PA: Destiny Image Publishers, Inc., 1991.

Webster's New Twentieth Century Dictionary of the English Language. New York, NY: Simon & Schuster, 1983.

Webster's New Universal Unabridged Dictionary. New York, NY: Barnes & Noble Books (with Random House Value Publishing, Inc.), 2003.

Wilson, Rufus Rockwell (ed.). "Intimate Memories of Lincoln" (Joshua F. Speed, 1880), as cited in *Abraham Lincoln and the Bible*. http://www.abrahamlincolnsclassroom.org/Library/newsletter.asp?ID=111&CRLI=159

Wolf, Fred Alan. *The Dreaming Universe: A Mind-Expanding Journey Into The Realm Where Psyche And Physics Meet*. New York, NY: Simon & Schuster, 1994.

Wylie, J.A. "The Dream of Elector Frederick the Wise." *History of Protestantism* Vol I. http://www.lutheranpress.com/fredericks_dream.htm

Zeiders, Charles. *Dreams and Christian Holism: Therapy and the Nocturnal Voice of God*. http://www.actheals.org/Publications/Full%20Reports/Clinical%20Inputs/06ClinicalDreams.pdf

About Judith A. Doctor

Author, speaker, mentor, Judith A. Doctor (MSW, RN) has helped many people rediscover dreams as gifts from God. Recognizing that we are missing a vital part of our heritage, she has contributed to the on-going restoration of this neglected aspect of Christian experience today.

Judith asserts that Christians need to reclaim a leadership role in bringing divine counsel and wisdom to our society through dreams. Her understanding of dreams comes from years of academic and personal study, her work in counseling others, and her own encounters with divine wisdom in her dreams.

In 2011 she wrote *Dream Treasure: Learning The Language Of Heaven*, a primer on understanding dreams from a Christian perspective. Her writing blends a combination of in-depth knowledge and personal experience.

Recently Judith authored *I Forgive You: How Heart-Based Forgiveness Sets You Free*. In addition, she has published in the *Journal of Christian Healing*, and in *Asociaţia De Nursing Din România Journal*.

Co-founder of Kairos Ministries, Inc., Judith conducts groups, retreats, and individual sessions for spiritual growth and healing in both the USA and Europe. Since 1980, she has addressed parish nurses, social workers, recovery groups, civic and social groups, German psychosomatic clinics, Romanian nurses, and numerous Christian groups, both Catholic and Protestant. Her ministry includes a monthly radio program live from Germany.

Judith enjoys chats with friends, evening rides, art exhibits, international mysteries, spiritual-political discourse, and morning coffee with her husband, Gerald. Married in 1959, they have two sons and daughters-in-law and four grandchildren.

Connect with Judith:
Blog – http://judithdoctor.com/blog
Facebook – https://www.facebook.com/JudithDoctor

Made in the USA
Coppell, TX
13 April 2021

53682528R00118